Science and Religions America

What is religion? What is science? How do they interact with each other? *Science and Religions in America: A New Look* offers a cutting-edge overview of the diverse range of religious traditions and their complex and fascinating interaction with science. Pluralistic in scope, the book is different from traditional Christian and/or monotheistic approaches to studying the rich interplay of religion and science in multi-religious American culture.

Featuring interviews with specialists in the field, Greg Cootsona draws on their insights to provide a comprehensive, accessible, and engaging introduction to the challenging interrelationship of religion and science. Each chapter focuses on a different religion within the United States, covering Buddhism, Christianity, Nature Religions, Islam, Judaism, Hinduism, and the Spiritual but Not Religious (SBNR).

Global religious traditions and their inextricable relationship with science and technology are examined in an accessible and interactive format. With "lightning round Q&As," contributions from leading thinkers, and suggestions for further reading, this book primes undergraduate students for studying the interchange of science and religions (in the plural) and is an exciting new resource for those interested in these topics in contemporary America.

Greg Cootsona is Lecturer in Comparative Religion and Humanities at California State University, Chico, USA. His most recent book is *Negotiating Science and Religion in America: Past, Present, and Future* (2019).

Science and Religions in America
A New Look

Greg Cootsona

LONDON AND NEW YORK

Designed cover image: Getty images—m-gucci #665875630

First published 2023
by Routledge
4 Park Square, Milton Park, Abingdon, Oxon OX14 4RN

and by Routledge
605 Third Avenue, New York, NY 10158

Routledge is an imprint of the Taylor & Francis Group, an informa business

© 2023 Greg Cootsona

British Library Cataloguing-in-Publication Data
A catalogue record for this book is available from the British Library

ISBN: 978-1-032-10211-5 (hbk)
ISBN: 978-1-032-10212-2 (pbk)
ISBN: 978-1-003-21423-6 (ebk)

DOI: 10.4324/9781003214236

Typeset in Bembo
by Apex CoVantage, LLC

To my past, present, and future science and religions students and to many others who share their interests

Contents

1 Why and how I think you should read this book—a bit of a roadmap

The first thing to tell you is why I wrote this book.

You see, I've been unsatisfied with what I've found in "science and religion" books. They strike me as incomplete because they are essentially "monotheism and science" or "Christianity and science." At some level, this is understandable and perhaps pardonable, given that the science commonly practiced derives from the European Scientific Revolution—which I'll call in these pages "modern science"—and that this European context was predominantly Christian. Nevertheless, as I've taught hundreds of students over the past two decades, I keep getting asked for a truly multi-religious approach to science. Why? There are, as I read in the National Congregations Study: "about as many synagogues, mosques and Buddhist or Hindu temples in the U.S. (9% of all congregations) as there are Catholic parishes (6% of all congregations)."[1]

We need to take in this religious diversity and its impact. Toni Morrison once wrote, "If there's a book that you want to read, but it hasn't been written yet, then you must write it."[2] And so, I'm writing this book because it doesn't exist yet, at least for use in my undergraduate courses at Chico State.

But it's not just for my students, and this leads to a relevant question, *Is this topic important to you too?* Not surprisingly, my answer is Yes, but it might not be evident why—almost all other vital cultural topics find their way through science and religions. When we look, for example, at the COVID-19 pandemic, discussions about race, or the contentiousness of evolution and climate change in the United States, we need to understand the cultural history of science and religion—and how the two are still intertwined.

This brings me to three phases of books written on science and religion.[3] The first phase focused on science and religion largely through western monotheism—and frankly, as I've mentioned, primarily through

DOI: 10.4324/9781003214236-1

Christianity and science. Ian Barbour's iconic game-changing 1966 book *Issues in Science and Religion*[4] set this agenda. Then, a second phase appeared, as in Alister McGrath's 2010 *Science and Religion: A New Introduction* (in its second edition, to be precise),[5] which I've used as textbook. This and other texts take up science and its relationship with western monotheism and then add a chapter or two on "other religions." Tipping their hats toward religious diversity, they still center on Christianity.

In my teaching, this seems inadequate, and my concerns are echoed in this summary from the *Stanford Encyclopedia of Philosophy*,

> For the past fifty years, science and religion has been de facto Western science and Christianity—to what extent can Christian beliefs be brought in line with the results of Western science? The field of science and religion has only recently turned to an examination of non-Christian traditions, such as Judaism, Hinduism, Buddhism, and Islam, providing a richer picture of interaction.[6]

I'd like to think this book is part of a third phase, exemplified by *Science and Religion Around the World*,[7] edited by John Hedley Brooke and Ronald L. Numbers, a truly decentered and pluralistic approach to religions and science. Like the authors in this collection, I am not assuming monotheism, morality, and its metaphysics (though, as an North American scholar, that bias is always close at hand). The book I've written is also a bit different in that it's for those who aren't specialists in the field of religion and science.

And this brings me back to my students and what they need and are asking for, as well as those readers who aren't college students in my Science and Religion course. I think you'll understand American life and better through studying science and religions (in the plural). The payoff here is that we gain insight into so many other topics.

One thing I'm not trying to do

I'm not setting out to write an extensive treatment of all that might be said about science and religion. I'm not covering, for example, Yoruba (as Stephen Prothero does in his fabulous book *God is Not One*).

What I do cover (in order) are Christianity, the Spiritual but Not Religious (SBNR), Buddhism, nature religions, Judaism, Islam, and Hinduism—ordered by their relative influence in the United States—all of which I've selected because of their influential presence in our country. And I suspect this focus will frustrate my scholarly peers who won't like that I don't entirely distinguish between Shia and Sunni Islam, or that

I pay insufficient attention to the varieties of Christianity, whether evangelical, Pentecostal, High Church Anglican, or liberal Catholic. Partly, this is practical—it is a by-product of the word length my publisher and I agreed on for this text.

It's also that I'm not sure these differences are worth wading through for you, the readers. I have also avoided other subtleties and shadings. I have generally decided not to add diacritical marks to words like *śūnyatā*, instead writing *shunyata* and even the *Quran* instead of the *Qur'an*. In this practice, I agree with Stephen Prothero when he concludes that "diacritical marks are gibberish to most readers . . . so I avoid them here except in direct quotations, proper names, and citations."[8]

Similarly, my endnotes are only references. I don't carry on a separate conversation there, which is a thing academics do, but almost all other readers find tiresome or extraneous. I have selected a half dozen books or so at the end of each chapter for further reading. They are, of course, not all the sources I've learned from. Those others you'll find in the endnotes.

I am also focusing on the present, not on the history of science and technology and a particular religion. My guideline is to include the history of each of the religious traditions only insofar as they directly influence the present engagement with science. For example, I would love to say something about the trial of Galileo Galilei—and specific mistakes made both by Galileo and by his antagonists—but that has been done elsewhere with clarity and insight, as in the brilliant set of essays, *Galileo Goes to Jail and Other Myths About Science and Religion*.[9] Instead, it's more important for me to focus on the way atheists deploy examples like these as evidence of the church's anti-science attitude and why that affects the way we understand Christianity's relationship with science today.

My overall hope is to present science and religions with the intent of fulfilling a kind of Academic Hippocratic Oath: *Do no harm*, to which I'll add, and, *seek to provide enough vocabulary for others to enter this conversation with competency*.

On a crash course with the study of religion

This book focuses on seven religions in the United States and how they relate to science. In other words, religion frames each chapter.

There are two related questions that I need to answer: (1) Why is religion so widespread? This is what the influential scholar of religion Huston Smith leaned into with his "perennial philosophy" approach in his bestselling *The World's Religions*.[10] Science, especially the Cognitive Science of Religion, and philosophy before that, has a response (though not entirely an "answer"). We are wired for religion. We are naturally religious. Each of us is the *homo religiosus* (2). And yet, why are religions so different? Prothero, as a kind of anti-Smith, emphasizes this pole.

Taking seriously these two questions—and the poles they lead to—I offer an approach spurred on by the 1984 book by Yale professor of religion and theology George Lindbeck, *The Nature of Doctrine*.[11] Lindbeck helped me to see religion within a "cultural–linguistic" approach. As the philosopher George Santayana phrased it,

> Any attempt to speak without speaking any particular language is not more hopeless than the attempt to have a religion that shall be no religion in particular . . . . Every living and healthy religion has a marked idiosyncrasy. Its power consists in its special and surprising message and the bias which that revelation gives to life.[12]

Lindbeck comments, "religions are seen as comprehensive interpretive schemes, usually embodied in myths or narratives and heavily ritualized, which structure human experience and understanding of self and world."[13]

This view reverses how we normally think of inner life and its outer expression. In the cultural–linguistic approach, outer forms inner. We start by understanding a religion's expression in community that then forms our personal experience: "a religious experience and its expression are secondary and tertiary in a linguistic-cultural model."[14] He adds, "different religions seem in many cases to produce fundamentally divergent depth experiences of what it is to be human."[15] In understanding another's religion, we must respect differences and not amalgamate them, or worse, make them sound just like ours. Prothero writes that religions "do converge when it comes to ethics, but they diverge sharply when it comes to doctrine, ritual, mythology, experience, and law."[16] To assert that they all ultimately are one is "dangerous, disrespectful, and untrue."[17]

I do agree that religions teach truths we need to verify—particularly when they come into conversation with science—and that there is a common spiritual seedbed. I've studied a number of languages, and this makes sense of what I've experienced. From my perspective, *interreligious work is fundamentally translation. One key goal in this book then is to present vocabulary and grammar for relating science and religions.*

Almost all religions—certainly even the classic five "world religions" of Judaism, Christianity, Islam, and Buddhism—all tolerate at best an uneasy relationship with the moniker *religion*. For example, Prothero has written, "One of the most common claims among Hindus in the West is that 'Hinduism is a way of life' rather than a religion . . . *Sanatana Dharma*

(Eternal Law),"[18] and many Christians will say that their faith is "a relationship, not a religion." Let me add that I do not equate religion with belief in a supernatural being. Buddhism, as is commonly known, has many nontheistic forms, and it is not even clear that the Buddha himself had much use for a god. That belief may, of course, be a component of religion in the sense that I'm using the word, but there's much more. The scholarly definition of *religion* brings us much closer to *spirituality* in common parlance, especially among emerging adults who play a major role in this book and my methods.

Quick and dirty definitions

With these considerations in mind, I arrive at my working definitions for three key terms. (By the way, these are the definitions I have adapted from various dictionaries and standard texts in the field, which have worked reasonably well. Still, there is nothing simple about this, and if you're interested, I go into more detail in the Conclusion.) First of all, *science* is "knowledge about or study of the natural world, framed in theories based on observation, which are tested through experimentation." Science studies nature. *Religion*, an even trickier term than science can be defined as "the belief in God or in many gods or Ultimate Reality, as well as an organized system of beliefs, ceremonies, sacred stories, and ethical guidelines used to relate to God, a plurality of gods, or Ultimate Reality." It includes what Prothero defines with four Cs: *creed* (belief), *code* (morals)*, cultus* (worship), and *community* (who you do these things with).[19] Finally, *technology* is "the use of science in industry, engineering, etc. to invent useful things or to solve problems" and "a machine, piece of equipment, method, etc., that is created by the use of science."[20]

Three—not four—ways to relate science and religion

Science is the great antagonist to the vitality of religion. At least that's a common assumption, and not without merit. As societies become more scientifically literate and technologically advanced, they tend to be less religious. Of course, it's not that simple, and the United States remains a highly religious and highly scientifically and technologically advanced country. Maybe there's more to be said. For that reason, I agree with journalist and radio talk show host, Steve Paulson, "Sorting out the relationship between science and religion *is* one of the great intellectual dramas of our time."[21]

Physicist-theologian Ian Barbour created a context for grasping how these two relate and his four-part typology has set the agenda for the study of science and religion. In his *Issues in Science and Religion*, Barbour set out four categories: *Conflict*, where each attacks the other as enemy; *Independence*, where each has a separate way of understanding; *Dialogue*, where there is polite discussion of insights; and *Integration*, where actual give-and-take and transformation takes place.

Many still employ Barbour's typology; I will simplify it a bit, particularly in excising his category of *dialogue*, which has always struck me as an uneasy midpoint on the road to integration (where, it seems, Barbour was really headed). Put simply, to dialogue is already to *integrate* at some level. Let me add that I've learned from U.C. San Diego sociologist John Evans, that, for most people, the relationship between science and religion is not about a "systematic knowledge conflict" between two elite groups (i.e., scientists and theologians), but more often about moral questions asked by the American populace.[22] Yet, one more nuance as we proceed.

Instead, I've found that a good place to start is by dividing how Americans relate science and religion into three main categories, *conflict, independent coexistence* (or *independence*), and *collaboration*. It also corresponds with a massive social scientific study of 10,541 participants by Elaine Howard Ecklund and Christopher Scheitle (more on that soon).

Conflict describes a state in which religion and science have never, and will never agree. Richard Dawkins certainly represents a key thought leader and perhaps the leading spokesperson of this type. Twenty-seven percent of American adults take this view (with 14% affirming "I'm on the side of religion" and 13%, "I'm on the side of science").[23] Consistent with these findings, some students I've interviewed and/or teach are hard-core adherents to the "warfare thesis" promoted in the late nineteenth century by such classic texts as Andrew Dickson White's *A History of the Warfare of Science with Theology in Christendom* and William Draper's also bestselling *History of the Conflict between Religion and Science*[24] (still two of the most widely read texts on science and religion) and contemporary books by Jerry Coyne and Richard Dawkins, as well as Philip Johnson and Ken Ham.[25]

The conflict model has remarkable staying power in popular culture, even if most scholars find it lacking.[26] As one student, Evelyn, commented in an interview with me, "I think that science and religion will always be in conflict because science and religion will never be able to agree, and there are such contradicting views."[27] If nothing else, there's a *perception* of conflict at the popular level. For example, conservative Protestants, who represent about 25% of the American populace, do see a conflict with science, and the media overrepresents their views because it is effective journalism.[28] Conflict sells, and in the process, warps.

Ecklund and Scheitle found that 35% of US adults hold a second view, *independent coexistence*, which understands religion and science as two completely different ways to look at the world that ought to remain separate. Stephen Jay Gould's Non-Overlapping Magisterial Authority (NOMA) is a frequent reference.[29] One of my Chico State students put this position with clarity: "Science is science, and religion is religion. Not much of a blend between the two."

Third, the largest slice of Americans in Ecklund and Scheitle's survey, at 38%, endorses an *integration* or *collaboration* of science and religion. Here I think of Pope Paul II's notable letter to the astronomer George Coyne, "Science can purify religion from error and superstition; religion can purify science from idolatry and false absolutes. Each can draw the other into a wider world, a world in which both can flourish."[30]

As you'll see in the pages that follow, the relationship between science and religion exists in all three modes. No one type that neatly summarizes American negotiation of science and religion. As the notable philosopher and mathematician Alfred North Whitehead once quipped "The guiding motto in the life of every natural philosopher should be, 'Seek simplicity and distrust it.'"[31] Similarly, the eminent historian of science and religion John Hedley Brooke presented his *complexity thesis*. That adjective *complex*—rather than warring or harmonious, or a host of others—best represents the way that science and religion have related, especially in our country. "Serious scholarship in the history of science has revealed so extraordinarily rich and complex a relationship between science and religion in the past that general theses are difficult to sustain. The real lesson turns out to be the complexity."[32]

Complexity and a dappled tapestry of relationships best portray how these two titanic forces interact. I am indeed indebted to Brooke's insight, even if it makes my job harder. It is much trickier to approach science and religion as more than a simple conflict or happy harmony.

The present moment in science

Each religion indeed has its own relationship with science. I am also focusing on these religions as they exist in the present, in other words, in the first half of the twenty-first century.

With that said, there are some topics, and forms of science, that religions cannot ignore. There are also some historical shifts that began in the nineteenth century: Charles Darwin's famous theory of evolution, the increase in a narrative of conflict between Christianity and science, and the emergence of deeper religious diversity through immigration to the United States.

I need to put my finger on that first topic. It is impossible for any religion not to figure out how to interact with biological evolution, and particularly Charles Darwin's 1859, *On the Origin of Species*. Darwin's theory, by itself, did lead to a universal conclusion that Christian faith and science were indelible foes. For one thing, though some rejected evolution, many leading Christian voices in the United States embraced the new theory. Still, the power of White's and Draper's rhetoric in the late nineteenth century, as well as voices like son-of-a-preacher-turned-atheist evangelist Robert Ingersoll, began to make it credible not to believe. Running alongside this narrative, various voices promoted Buddhism as a more science-friendly religion.

A bit later, physics, which loomed even more prominently 100 years ago, still presents its own story of the universe and its origins as well as its rendering of basic reality. Albert Einstein's special and general theories of relativity in the first decades of the twentieth century, and the quantum revolution in the early 1920s—and its counter-intuitive conclusions about matter and energy that Einstein resisted—are challenges, and to some, promises—either thrown down or laid invitingly at the feet of religious practitioners and leaders. Additionally, neuroscience and cognitive science have posed significant questions about traditional religious concepts like the soul. Climate change, as an ethical issue, looms large, and every religion has to figure out its response. Those are all significant topics, and each religion adds its own favorite, or feared, scientific disciplines. With all that to consider, I did not have enough space to address with any sustained attention the COVID-19 pandemic.

Final thoughts

I hope this doesn't sound grandiose, but living and teaching in California have placed me in one of the most diverse religious environments in the United States. In the Golden State, we run the gamut—from the megachurches of Southern California, both historically and contemporarily (Aimee Sample McPherson's Angelus Temple, Robert Schuller's Crystal Cathedral, Rick Warren's Saddleback Church) to one of the most non-religious area of our country (Silicon Valley), to significant minority religions like Sikhs in the northern part of our state, and to robust Buddhist and Hindu population centers in Southern California and the San Francisco Bay Area.

I happen to think that relating science and religions remains a critical, and essentially unfinished, task for us in the twenty-first century because almost every issue we face is either directly related to these two cultural forces or at least affected by this dialogue. These two also open us to just about every joy we can experience. In unfolding Native science, biologist Gregory Cajete comments, "the more humans know about themselves— that is, their connections with everything around them—the greater the celebration of life, the greater the comfort of knowing, and the greater joy of being."[33] That seems accurate to me.

I've subtitled this chapter "A Bit of a Roadmap" because to encounter the interplay of science and religion is to begin an excursion. I hope you'll enjoy the journey in this book.

Suggestions for further reading

To grasp the contours of most of the religions addressed in this book, the two classics (described in this chapter) are Huston Smith's wise and engaging *The World's Religions* (New York: HarperSanFrancisco, 1991), first published as *The Religions of Man* in 1958; and more recently, the winsomely written book by Stephen Prothero, *God Is Not One: The Eight Rival Religions That Run the World* (New York: HarperOne, 2010). For a quick tour of modern science, I have returned repeatedly to Timothy Ferris, *Coming of Age in the Milky Way* (New York: HarperCollins, 2003), and Lawrence M. Principe, *The Scientific Revolution: A Very Short Introduction* (Oxford: Oxford University Press, 2011).

There are several excellent books on science and religion. Here are just four. For a multi-religious approach, check out the edited collection from John Hedley Brooke and Ronald L. Numbers, *Science and Religion Around the World* (Oxford: Oxford University Press, 2011). For a pair of very reliable introductions, it's hard to go wrong with Philip Clayton's *Religion and Science: The Basics*, 2nd ed. (New York: Routledge, 2018) and Alister McGrath's *Science and Religion*—the newest edition is the 3rd (Oxford: Wiley-Blackwell, 2020). And because of its focus on the United States, I'm going to include my text: Cootsona, *Negotiating Science and Religion in America: Past, Present, and Future* (London: Routledge, 2019).

Notes

1 National Congregations Study, "Congregations in 21st Century America," https://sites.duke.edu/ncsweb/files/2022/02/NCSIV_Report_Web_FINAL2.pdf, accessed 16 September 2022.

2 Ellen Brown, "Writing Is Third Career for Morrison," 27 September 1981, *The Cincinnati Enquirer*, www.newspapers.com/clip/21863475/tonimorrison, accessed 8 July 2022.

3 Much of this follows George Lindbeck's brilliant analysis in *The Nature of Doctrine: Religion and Theology in a Postliberal Age* (Philadelphia, PA: Westminster Press, 1984).

4 Barbour, *Issues in Science and Religion* (Hoboken, NJ: Prentice-Hall, 1966).

5 McGrath, *Science and Religion: A New Introduction*, 2nd ed. (Oxford: Wiley-Blackwell, 2010). The 2020 revised third edition has no chapters dedicated to other religions. Another example is Christopher Southgate, gen. ed., *God, Humanity, and the Cosmos: A Textbook in Science and Religion*, 3rd ed. (London: T & T Clark, 2011).

6 "Religion and Science," *Stanford Encyclopedia of Philosophy*, https://plato.stanford.edu/entries/religion-science, accessed 16 June 2022.

7 John Hedley Brooke and Ronald L. Numbers, eds., *Science and Religion Around the World* (Oxford: Oxford University Press, 2011).

8 Prothero, *God Is Not One: The Eight Rival Religions That Run the World* (New York: HarperOne, 2010), "A Note on Dates and Diacriticals."

9 Ronald L. Numbers, *Galileo Goes to Jail and Other Myths About Science and Religion* (Cambridge, MA: Harvard University Press, 2010).

10 Huston Smith, *The World's Religions* (New York: HarperSanFrancisco, 1991).

11 George Lindbeck, *The Nature of Doctrine: Religion and Theology in a Postliberal Age* (Philadelphia, PA: Westminster Press, 1984).

12 George Santayana, *Reason in Religion*, cited by Clifford Geertz, *The Interpretation of Cultures* (New York: Basic Books, 1973), 87.

13 Lindbeck, 32.

14 Ibid., 39.

15 Ibid., 41.

16 Ibid., 3.

17 Ibid.

18 Ibid., 135.

19 Prothero, 325.

20 Merriam-Webster Dictionary, s.v. "technology," definition for English Language Learners, www.merriam-webster.com/dictionary/technology, accessed 21 May 2019.

21 Paulson, *Atoms and Eden: Conversations on Religion and Science* (Oxford: Oxford University Press, 2010), 1.

22 See, for example, Evans, *Morals Not Knowledge: Recasting the Contemporary U.S. Conflict Between Religion and Science* (Berkeley, CA: University of California Press, 2018), 84.

23 Elaine Howard Ecklund and Christopher Scheitle, *Religion vs. Science: What Religious People Really Think* (Oxford: Oxford University Press, 2018), 64, summarized in Table 4.4.

24 Andrew Dickson White, *A History of the Warfare of Science with Theology in Christendom* (Cambridge: Cambridge University Press, 2009 [1896]) and William Draper's also best-selling *History of the Conflict Between Religion and Science* (Cambridge: Cambridge University Press, 2009 [1875]).

25 Philip Johnson, *Darwin on Trial*, 20th anniversary ed. (Downers Grove, IL: IVP Books, 2010), and Ken Ham, Answers in Genesis, https://answersingenesis.org, accessed 16 June 2022.

26 Jeff Hardin, Ronald L. Numbers, and Ronald A. Binzley, eds., *The Warfare Between Science and Religion: The Idea That Wouldn't Die* (Baltimore, MD: Johns Hopkins University Press, 2018) and Ronald L. Numbers, ed., *Galileo Goes to Jail and Other Myths About Science and Religion* (Cambridge, MA: Harvard University Press, 2010). For a wider context, see also Gary B. Ferngren, *Science and Religion: A Historical Introduction* (Baltimore, MD: Johns Hopkins, 2002); David C.

Lindberg and Ronald L. Numbers, eds., *Where Science and Christianity Meet* (Chicago, IL: University of Chicago Press, 2003); Thomas Dixon, Geoffrey Cantor, and Stephen Pumfrey, eds., *Science and Religion: New Historical Perspectives* (Cambridge: Cambridge University Press, 2010). On the other side of the ledger, there are some adherents in scholarly work, e.g., Roland Bénabou, Davide Ticchi, and Andrea Vindigni, "Forbidden Fruits: The Political Economy of Science, Religion, and Growth," 2013, www.princeton.edu/~rbenabou/papers/Religion%20 December%201g_snd.pdf, accessed 23 June 2019), the conflict thesis is prevalent in popular treatments, e.g., Jerry Coyne, *Faith Versus Fact: Why Science and Religion Are Incompatible* (New York: Penguin, 2016), 2015, and Richard Dawkins, *The God Delusion* (New York: Mariner, 2008).

27 These quotes from students, and those that follow, are all taken from my qualitative interviews partly for the Science for Students and Emerging Young Adults (SEYA) project, but also for continuing personal research, www.templeton.org/grant/science-for-students-and-emerging-young-adults-seya, accessed 16 June 2022.

28 John Evans, in Hardin, Numbers, and Binzley, eds., *The Warfare Between Science and Religion*, 330ff.

29 A quite short, but entirely useful version can be found here: Stephen Jay Gould, "Nonoverlapping Magisteria," *Natural History* 106 (1997): 16–22.

30 Pope John Paul II, quoted in Robert John Russell, William R. Stoeger, and George V. Coyne, eds., *Physics, Philosophy, and Theology* (Notre Dame, IN: University of Notre Dame Press, 1988), 13.

31 A. N. Whitehead, *The Concept of Nature* (Cambridge: Cambridge University Press, 1920), 46.

32 Brooke, 5.

33 Cajete, *Native Science*, 75.

2 Complex and frequently misunderstood

Christianity and science

"The God of the Bible is also the God of the genome. He can be worshiped in the cathedral or the laboratory."[1] When Francis Collins—whose resume includes serving as Principal Investigator of the Human Genome Initiative, as head of the National Institutes of Health, and as Science Advisor to the President—declares the compatibility of his faith with modern science, it might appear that the relationship of Christianity with science is as placid as a mountain lake on a windless day.

Naturally, all is not that smooth. Christianity suffers from bad press, which regularly proclaims, "Christianity is anti-science." And yet, if anything fits into the *complexity thesis*, presented by the leading historian of religion and science John Hedley Brooke, it is this religion.

Because of its prominence, Christianity's relationship with science is also the most given over to slogans, memes, and stereotypes. And in my view, all this makes the relationship between Christianity and science fascinating. I could call this then a "relationship defining" chapter. How do Christianity and science actually relate? How can one religion provoke such divergent responses? The topic of this chapter is prone to preconceptions more than any other in this book, specifically that science and Christian belief are locked in a titanic battle. Here, sociologists Elaine Howard Ecklund and Christopher Scheitle offer a calm, measured overview that holds for monotheist faiths generally, but certainly for Christianity specifically,

> For example, contrary to the stereotypes that religious Americans are hostile to science, we find that they are interested in and appreciate science. Yet people of faith, particularly the Christians, Muslims, and Jews we study here, view science through the lens of concern about keeping a place for an active God in the world.[2]

DOI: 10.4324/9781003214236-2

I have to start our journey with science and religions here because the Christian church is still the biggest player in the United States. It will remain that way for quite a while, despite the market share it's lost. Put another way, it is not quite against the ropes, though it's taken a few punches in the past few decades.

Introducing Christianity: a lightning round Q & A

Even if Christianity is the largest and probably the most diverse religion in the world, let me provide a brief overview through a lightning round of question and answer.

Following Stephen Prothero's structure for understanding any religion,[3] *what is the problem and what is the solution that Christianity presents?*

"Saved from sin" is essentially Prothero's problem–solution model for Christianity. We are separated from God, one another, and creation, and we are redeemed in Jesus Christ. This isn't wrong entirely and may be a good starting point.

What does the name "Christian" mean?

Followers of Jesus the Christ, derive their name title comes from the Greek *christos*, which means Messiah. In the Bible, the name "Christian" is first used in the New Testament in Acts 11:26 to refer to followers of Jesus.

Where was it founded?

Southern Levant (modern-day Israel, Palestine, and Jordan)

When did it start?

Probably best to start the movement at 33 CE with the death, by the capital punishment of crucifixion, of Jesus of Nazareth, whose followers (or disciples) quickly pronounced that he had been resurrected on the third day after his death.

What are the three primary branches of Christianity?

Roman Catholic, Eastern Orthodox, and Protestant.

What are common spiritual practices?

Prayer, baptism, Eucharist or (Communion), Bible study, and Sunday worship services.

What are the main holy days?

Christmas, the celebration of Jesus's birth, and Easter, the celebration of his resurrection.

How many Christians in the world?

Somewhere around 25% of the world population or 2.2 billion.

How many Christians are scientists in the United States?

According to the Pew Report, around 30% of scientists identify as Christians,[4] and, as a related fact, Christians have received almost two-thirds of Physics Nobel prizes.[5]

Ted Peters: scholar and guide for this chapter

To guide me in this chapter, I talked with Lutheran theologian and leading voice in the dialogue of science and theology. Ted Peters is Emeritus Professor of Systematic Theology and Ethics at Pacific Lutheran Theological Seminary and the Graduate Theological Union (GTU) as well as the world-renowned Center for Theology and the Natural Sciences. His interests range from quantum physics and the doctrine of creation to the implications of genetics for understanding what it means to be human to the implications of extraterrestrial life for Christian theology. Among the titles from his prodigious output, I've enjoyed *God—the World's Future, Playing God? Genetic Determinism and Human Freedom*, and *Astrotheology: Science and Theology Meet Extraterrestrial Life*. It is impossible to summarize all he's done in this field, and so I'll simply say this: Ted was my dissertation advisor (or *Doctorvater*) at the GTU and has been a longtime mentor and friend. He is a great storyteller, and that's appropriate because he's been part of the narrative of science and religion for the past 60 years or so. Let me start there.

Two initial caveats

I begin with this warning: Many Christian thinkers founded the sixteenth- and seventeenth-century European Scientific Revolution, which means that the relationship between science and religion in North American and European contexts often implicitly means "Christianity and science." Conversely, when atheists and agnostics fought against the religious establishment—whether in the eighteenth-century French Enlightenment or in the late-nineteenth-century Anglo-American context or today—all are taking on Christianity. This naturally biases all considerations of the topic at hand.

Second, wisdom suggests that we ponder this line from Stephen Prothero:

> There is a persistent, unexplored bias in the study of religion toward the extraordinary and away from the ordinary. In the United States this bias manifests in a strong attraction (even among scholars who are atheists) toward hardcore religious practitioners.[6]

Nowhere is this more applicable than with Christianity, where too often the loudest and most strident voice are the fundamentalists', with their cavils against "godless" evolution and the climate change "hoax," while millions of believers have no significant problems with either one. Though this approach makes good copy for the media—and it's not absolute fiction—it won't focus there because I want to bring out the nuance.

Christianity is the largest religion in the world and therefore the most diverse. Despite my best efforts, this chapter is a bit longer than the others for that reason. Still, though I have spent more of my academic study on this religion than on any other, I do not intend to speak for all Christians. Instead, I can sketch a picture that reasonably represents how Christianity, overall, relates to science.

A little bit of history

I've asked Peters from his experience about the way the modern study of religion, or theology, and science emerged. He offered this starting with his dissertation advisor from the University of Chicago,

> Langdon Gilkey, with whom I studied in the 1960s, was doing science and culture, and he believed in what Ian Barber called the Independence View or the two-language views. Science is over here. Religions over there. And the two of them never get together. What Ian Barber did in 1966 with his book, *Issues in Science or Religion*, was to point out that there are many places where theology and science need to hook together. And then in the 1970s, that was picked up in England by John Polkinghorne at Cambridge and Arthur Peacock at Oxford.

But, I asked, what about the work he did in Berkeley?

> In 1980, Bob Russell and Ian Barbour gave us their vision for the Center for Theology and Natural Sciences. By the 1980s it was Ian Barber's agenda, which came to dominate the field. The first big

issues were methodology: How do we know things? Are scientific knowledge and theological knowledge similar or different?

Is there more? "In physics, there was so much excitement about the Copenhagen interpretation of the electron and the photon being indeterministic. How will that affect a theological thinking if we no longer live in a strictly mechanistic universe." And we will get to the topic. And then as an afterthought, he added "and of course, Big Bang cosmology." But let's return to the first part first. *How do science and religion approach the world? How do we bring together faith and reason?*

Faith and reason

One of the most common criticisms from scientific atheists lies here. "Science is about evidence. Faith is about having none, but believing anyway." I often hear that slogan from my college students, and it continues to dominate many classroom discussions and social media posts. If they didn't think of it themselves, they may have evolutionary biologist and atheist Richard Dawkins to thank, who regularly produces quotable quips: "Faith means blind trust, in the absence of evidence even in the teeth of evidence."[7] Or to paraphrase Mark Twain, faith is "believing what you know ain't true."[8]

Of course, these challenges aren't without merit: the faith of theistic religions (Christianity included, of course) looks to an unseen, immaterial reality, God, while science seeks to understand the material workings of the natural world. Partly, this is the essential difference between many religions and science (one looks at God, the other analyzes the cause and effect within the natural world), and it reminds us to keep a healthy ingredient of independence between the two. As Galileo Galilei once retorted, "I would say here something that was heard from an ecclesiastic of the most eminent degree: 'That the intention of the Holy Ghost is to teach us how one goes to heaven, not how heaven goes.'"[9]

Accordingly, I need to define *faith*, a virtue emphasized by the monotheism, as in Christianity (but also Judaism and Islam). Often misunderstood and misrepresented, it essentially means reliance, fidelity, or trust (exemplified in the key New Testament Greek word *pistis*). Certainly, there are believers who have faith *despite* the evidence, but C.S. Lewis, whose book *Mere Christianity* still sells to millions and guides their understanding of the Christian faith, wrote that faith is "the art of holding on to things your reason has once accepted, in spite of your changing moods."[10] Faith in this case is *fiduciary*, holding on to sacred values, and a relationship with one's Creator. Faith is faithfulness to our commitments, which exists at the heart of Christianity.

Historically, the relationship between Christian faith and science does not only include antagonism, but more often, nurture. A reasonable faith (like the one Lewis presented, but of course present in many others) provides the seedbed for the rise of modern science in sixteenth- and seventeenth-century Europe.[11] Of course, scientific endeavors flourished in the eighth to fourteenth centuries in Muslim countries (a topic in another chapter), but that actually further substantiates this connection of monotheism with the rise of science as we know it today. This approach to faith, to state it ever so succinctly, is one reason the Scientific Revolution occurred in Christian Europe. Faith in the God who creates implies an ordered creation to study, analyze, or put simply, look at scientifically. As the Nobel Laureate UC Berkeley physicist Charles Townes once noted, "For successful science of the type we know, we must have faith that the universe is governed by reliable laws and, further, that these laws can be discovered by human inquiry."[12]

Creation and evolution

Creation versus evolution *is* the knee-jerk topic of Christianity and science. Alternatively set in a simple dichotomy, "God or Darwin." As a first-year undergraduate named Liz told me in an interview,

> I grew up in a religious household where we prayed before every meal and went to church every Sunday. I was fed the knowledge of the Bible and what it stood for. I never questioned my religious beliefs because I was taught not to. As a result, I grew up believing in something I didn't want to believe in. However, when the theory of evolution was brought to my attention I began to stop believing.

Polling data in the United States seems to support it: "Around four-in-ten white evangelical Protestants (38 percent) say humans have always existed in their present form," according to a summary by the Pew Report in 2019, "and about a quarter (27 percent) of black Protestants share this view." These are sizable percentages, but not the whole story. As I mentioned earlier, I will not resort solely to the most conservative voices because the actual relationship of their faith with evolutionary science is more varied than these stereotypes. Eighty-nine percent of American Catholics and 86% of mainline Protestants support evolution. In sum, most Christians are not young-earth or old-earth creationists and have concluded that God can work through the evolutionary process.[13]

This was true even when Charles Darwin first presented his views in 1859: It wasn't only conflict—though that certainly existed. For every

British cleric like Samuel Wilberforce and American evangelist Billy Sunday who rejected Darwin, there was Asa Gray, the Harvard botanist and evangelical Christian who promoted Darwin's theories in America as well as Charles Kingsley, who found edifying wisdom in evolution, "We knew of old that God was so wise that He could make all things; but behold, He is so much wiser than even that, that He can make all things make themselves."[14]

Of course, the interpretation of biblical texts, such as Genesis 1, is critical. Did God create in six literal 24-hour days, or is there something else that these texts have to say about God's act of creation? It doesn't seem to be about God as Creator *per se*, or as Peters phrased it by way of comparison, "Jewish scientists were the first ones to engage with Darwinian evolution, etc. So, I don't think it's an issue about a monotheistic God." And let it not be missed that having a definitive scriptural revelation of God creating the world presents these issues. As I note in a later chapter, Hindus generally accept evolutionary theory because they are fluid in their interpretations of sacred texts. The same kind of conflict does not exist there.

Centrally, it is about how to interpret the Bible, and the answer of how to connect modern science and God's creation results in four major perspectives.[15] The young-earth creationists like Ken Ham and Todd Wood proclaim that the earth is 6,000–10,000 years old. Old-earth creationists like Hugh Ross hold to a reasonable standard view of cosmic evolutionary time but reject biological evolution, while many Christians hold to Intelligent Design theory, which asserts that the complexity of life forms today cannot be the result of undirected process and present a variety of views on the age of the Earth. The perspective that most closely aligns itself with the scientific consensus, and is held by most Christians, is a theistic evolution or "evolutionary creation," a position ably represented by Collins.[16]

What about the related question of a historical Adam and Eve? Elsewhere, I've outlined three major positions.[17] First, young-earth creationists maintain that God specially created the historical pair, Adam and Eve, in the Garden of Eden. A second position accepts standard evolutionary science but maintains that a historical Adam and Eve existed within the development of human beings.[18] Others, like Lewis, propose a third position: a literal Adam and Eve never existed, and instead that they are paradigmatic of the human condition. Lewis wrote, "For long centuries, God perfected the animal form which was to become the vehicle of humanity and the image of himself."[19] Given this approach, we are not descended from one pair, but from the gradual evolutionary development of hominins. *Hominin* represents "the group consisting of modern humans, extinct human species and all our immediate ancestors (including members of genera *Homo*, *Australopithecus*, *Paranthropus*, and *Ardipithecus*)."[20] In addition, according to evolutionary theory, great apes and humans arose from a single ancestral species that existed in the distant past.

If the theme is coming through that the tradition of Christian religion is wide and allows for a variety of ways to engage with science, then I'm making my point.

CSR and the origins of belief

When I talked with Peters about the history of science and religion, he told me that in the late 1990s, "the new kid on the block" was the topic of neuroscience. It emerged as a key contribution to the field and shows no signs of retreating.

Especially, one amazing outgrowth of evolutionary thought is the way in which natural selection has formed our brains to be religious in forming groups and in leading us to believe in a supernatural being or beings,[21] as described by Justin Barrett and Pascal Boyer, who are two leaders in the growing field of the Cognitive Science of Religion (CSR).[22] CSR "investigates how human cognitive systems inform and constrain religious thought, experience, and expression."[23] Barrett writes that it "is probably best known for its efforts to explain broad, cross-cultural questions concerning why people generally tend to be religious throughout history and around the globe."[24] Put another way, CSR reveals that our brain's structure leads us toward a desire for more than this world has to offer and thus belief in God or gods.

Furthermore, CSR adapts the findings of the cognitive sciences to argue that evolution has developed human beings so that we implicitly see purposes in events or are predisposed toward teleology. This is also called "Hyperactive Agency Detection." Simply put, "Evidence exists that people are prone to see the world as purposeful and intentionally ordered," which naturally leads to belief in a Creator. For example, preschoolers "are inclined to see the world as purposefully designed and tend to see an intelligent, intentional agent behind this natural design."[25]

Similarly, neuroscientists Andrew Newberg and Eugene D'Aquili, in studying human brain activity, found a remarkable cognitive function that supports belief in God, thereby answering the question *Why God Won't Go Away*.[26] Robert McCauley, in his counterintuitively titled book *Why Religion is Natural and Science is Not*, demonstrates that the practices of religion (such as story and ritual) are comfortable or "natural" to our brains, while the hard, analytic work of scientific investigation is not.[27]

Whether the insights of cognitive science lead to a conclusion that "we are wired to believe in God" or "God created us this way so that we are open to belief" divides the practitioners of CSR and represents one more science-religion flashpoint.

The Big Bang

The Big Bang and the Anthropic Principle seem to offer support, respectively, for Christian teachings of creation out of nothing and God's intention to create. In interviewing undergraduates for a study project on emerging adult attitudes about religion and science, Christina told me this: "Science and nature was fascinating for me. I wondered why things happened. How we have what we have? I love watching things grow. It opened all kinds of questions. How did this get created?"

Though these two appear to present astounding convergence with Christianity, the reality, again, remains much more complicated.

Let's start at the beginning (as it were). Traditionally, Christians believe in creation out of nothing (or *creatio ex nihilo* in Latin). God didn't order a universe that was already there, nor did God and nature coexist. Instead, God is entirely sovereign over the heavens and the earth. As Psalm 33:9 states succinctly, "For [God] spoke and it came to be."

And this seems to connect with Big Bang cosmology, an extrapolation of Albert Einstein's theory of general relativity, first presented in 1915, which pointed to a universe that isn't static (in contrast to what Einstein would have liked). Instead, relativity implied that the universe is expanding. When expansion is extrapolated in reverse, this implies an initial singularity where time began, or $t = 0$. This is the "day without yesterday," where space was infinitely curved and all energy and all matter were concentrated into a single quantum.[28] The expanding cone of the universe has a point at one end, and that point is where we can locate the Big Bang.

The Belgian Jesuit priest and mathematician George Lemaitre and Edwin Hubble, the virtuoso of astronomical investigation, had to convince Einstein otherwise. Einstein, however, was not the only scientist in need of persuasion. In 1948, the brilliant Cambridge astronomer Fred Hoyle presented the reigning view of the time "steady state" cosmology with two colleagues, Herman Bondi and Thomas Gold. Simply put, the universe was virtually unchanging and of infinite age. "Unlike the modern school of cosmologists, who in conformity with Judeo-Christian theologians believe the whole universe to have been created out of nothing, my beliefs accord with those of Democritus who remarked 'Nothing is created out of nothing.'"[29] Hoyle argued forcefully for his theory and disparaged the alternative with a slight—the "Big Bang."

These two theories contended for scientific approval. It was not until 1965 that Robert Wilson and Arno Penzias of the Bell Laboratories detected background static radiation in the cosmos. This static was so unexpected that Wilson and Penzias believed pigeons had roosted in their enormous instruments. In fact, the pigeons had made a home there and even left some droppings. Once all that was purged, the background static remained nevertheless. It was the "echoes" of that initial explosive moment of the Big Bang. The COBE satellite probed outer space in 1989 and found further confirmation of this background radiation through its Far Infrared Absolute Spectrophotometer.

There are other competing forms of scientific cosmology that upend Big Bang. Scientists and atheist Lawrence Krauss (whose atheism, like Hoyle's, is a relevant fact in this case) recently presented one alternative to divine creation based on the effects of quantum "nothingness."[30] Here, it's important to underline that quantum nothingness is not really the absence of existence. In classical Christian thought, *creatio ex nihilo* is that there was no thing, not even quantum nothingness, "before" creation. (I set "before" in quotation marks because God's creation of the world also started time. So there really isn't a temporal "before" and "after.")

At any rate, Big Bang cosmology holds the current consensus and also seems to provide consonance with Paul's words in Romans 4:17, about the God "calls into being things that were not" and thus creation *ex nihilo*. The leading astronomer Robert Jastrow certainly thought so. He offered these hyperbolic comments on the Big Bang cosmology with a view to Genesis 1–3, "A sound explanation may exist for the explosive birth of our Universe; but if it does, science cannot find out what the explanation is. The scientist's pursuit of the past ends in the moment of creation." Jastrow could have stopped there, but he continues with some reasonably grandiose statements that a Christian evangelist might proclaim—and yet Jastrow was agnostic! "This is an exceedingly strange development, unexpected by all but the theologians. They have always accepted the word of the Bible: In the beginning God created heaven and earth."[31]

I quote this because it's enjoyable. But it's also hyperbole. Whether to have a "beginning" means to be "created,"[32] or whether t = 0 is really the initial act of creation, or whether it's one in a cycle of expansion and contractions, have not been resolved.

Fine-tuning

Still, this Big Bang also appears to be an extremely precise event. And this leads us to *cosmic fine-tuning* or the *Anthropic Principle*.[33] Since the 1960s, when scientists begun to identify discrete, precisely calibrated parameters that produced the universe we know, these particularly allow for the emergence of conscious, moral creatures. "Anthropic" comes from the Greek word for human being, *anthropos*, and states that the universe is fitted from its inception for the emergence of life in general and intelligent, moral life in particular, though not necessarily earthly carbon-based life or *Homo sapiens*.[34]

These perfectly calibrated, fine-tuned parameters have led many believers to nod in agreement with Freeman Dyson, the physicist who has spent many years at Princeton's famed Institute for Advanced Study, "The more I examine the universe and the details of its architecture, the more evidence I find that the universe in some sense most have known we are coming."[35] For some, this is a decisive victory for God's creation and against the common atheistic assertion that we are the products of blind, random, impersonal forces.

But does fine-tuning truly offer evidence in the structure of creation for this to be the fingerprint of God? Here's where it's easy to overstate the case. Some present the multiverse theory as a rejoinder—in other words, there have been innumerable attempts at other universes, which simply failed. Many, like the astronomer Owen Gingrich, consider this theory metaphysical speculation because it is, in principle, inaccessible to our scientific verification.[36] I turn to philosophy directly and the strongest argument against fine-tuning as a proof of God's creation: it's a tautology. Simply put, we are here in this particular universe. Whether its existence is perfectly calibrated or not, it's the only universe we've got. In a sense, that makes the probability of its existence 100%. Similarly, it's just as intrinsically improbable that a person named Greg is typing on a MacBook pro at his home in Chico on the fine-tuning argument because he's thinking about the doctrine of creation and science, etc. But yet here I am. And we don't offer that set of data as evidence for a Designer.

Alister McGrath, Oxford's professor of theology and science offers this assessment. The cosmological factors highlighted by cosmic fine-tuning don't offer "irrefutable evidence for the existence or character of a creator God." Instead he writes, "They are consistent with a theistic worldview; that they reinforce the plausibility with the greatest ease within such a worldview; that they reinforce the plausibility of such a worldview for those who are already committed to them."[37]

Peters reminded me that there is one addition to the Anthropic Principle besides the multiverse, Astrotheology (a revision of theology in light of the possibility of extraterrestrial life) and Astroethics. Even within the universe we know, more than 5,000 exoplanets (planets outside our solar system)[38] produce their own counterargument. *If God is so specially interested in human beings that God becomes a man, what about other planets where there is life, but no human beings?* Indeed, some say that the existence of exoplanets and extraterrestrial life (ETs) invalidates the Christian faith. A *HuffPost* blog piece, "Earth 2.0: Bad News for God" states it clearly:

> Let us be clear that the Bible is unambiguous about creation: the earth is the center of the universe, only humans were made in the image of god, and all life was created in six days. . . . Life on another planet is completely incompatible with religious tradition. Any other conclusion is nothing but ex-post facto rationalization to preserve the myth.[39]

Peters, with the help of a graduate student Julie Froehlig, decided to see give this an empirical test, and they conducted the Peters ETI Religious Crisis survey.[40]

> There were ten questions in this survey, and here's one that's particularly interesting. The question goes something like this, "If we were to make contact with an extraterrestrial intelligent civilization you think? Would the religions of the world suffer a crisis and collapse?" The ones who said yes to that were the nonreligious. But those people self-identified as religious don't think so.

Several decades earlier, Lewis, an avid amateur astronomer as well as a Renaissance scholar, mounted a telescope on the balcony of his bedroom at his home near Oxford, The Kilns. His love for the stars led him to ponder these questions and concluded that a good God could have created life on other planets. Lewis challenged the assumption that these creatures would be "fallen" in the same way human beings are and thus in need of redemption.[41] Moreover, he knew from his study of the history or thought that medieval and Enlightenment Christian thinkers had already pondered intelligent beings outside our Earth, finding no ultimate theological problem.

Peters is also not troubled about Christian belief and extraterrestrial life. In fact, in his book *Astrotheology*, he argued that a creative God could create other life forms that respond with conscious praise.[42]

In sum, it's clear to me that ETs impugn a conservative reading of the Christian redemptive scheme, but not all.

Technology and Christianity

Technology creates something through the application of science, and this has been part of humankind for quite a while. In particular, the Christian church and technology have enjoyed a long and often positive history.

Scholars have noted that the early Christian church spread the use of the codex, or book, as opposed to the scroll. Try to find a particular chapter in the Bible on a scroll, and not by looking at page 432, and you'll quickly see why this is significant. Without its scholarship as we know it would hardly exist. And speaking of books, in another chapter, I noted the lesser-known emergence of printing in Buddhism in the ninth century CE. Nevertheless, many of us know of Johannes Gutenberg's press, developed around 1,440, that allowed Martin Luther to print pamphlets to spread the Protestant Reformation. Not only that, but Luther and Calvin's emphasis on reading the Bible in common language depended on the printing press. It was so much cheaper than scribes' copying manuscripts that more people were able to obtain their own Bibles. It's no wonder that the most famous book from Johannes Gutenberg's technological advance was the Gutenberg Bible. Today, Internet technology has promoted the expansion of the Bible even further (e.g., YouVersion).

Of course, Christianity's relationship with technology is not all positive. Strong Artificial Intelligence increasingly offers examples for machines that seem to have a soul, which traditionally has been reserved for humans only. The film *Ex Machina* presents one of its key characters, Nathan, a computer genius and owner of a web-search company. (Think Google.) Nathan creates Ava, a beautiful and alluring strong artificial intelligence (AI) robot. During the film, Nathan declares something significant to Caleb (one of his employees who has been recruited by Nathan to assess Ava): "The arrival of strong artificial intelligence has been inevitable for decades. The variable was when, not if."

Strong AI presses the question of *What is the soul?* especially because it increasingly replicates what traditional theological definitions of the soul have presented. Christian thought—when it's not influenced by Platonism's division of soul and body—endorses a human psychosomatic (soul–body) unity. This, of course, demonstrates the indelible imprint of Jewish thought on Christianity. In Genesis 2:7, God created the first man, *adam*, from the dust, *adamah*, by breathing in his breath. Body and soul are unified, even if at death, they will be unnaturally separated until they are reunited at the final resurrection.

I packed a considerable amount of Christian teaching in that last brief paragraph, but my point is this: Christian doctrine generally holds to a soul that is united with the body, one that is not solely material. By way of contrast, Buddhism, with its teaching of *anatman* or no-soul, has a much easier path to tread with contemporary neuroscience that seems to find no soul apart from our brain's activity. Whether or not the findings of neuroscience can actually discern some non-material is, naturally, a critical question.

Science and Christian ethics

Recently, I was talking with my colleague, friend, and pastor-theologian Dr. Edgardo Rosado, who told me, "Many Latinos drive trucks. And, in the next ten years, those jobs will be lost to Artificial Intelligence. I want to help train my church not to lose their jobs to AI, but instead to create AI." The effects of technology and science often displace jobs, and so we arrive at justice, one of the ethical foundations of Christianity (which it, of course, adapts from its Jewish roots).

Many believers see Christianity, like many other religions do, as a way of life, not ultimately as intellectual content. UC San Diego sociologist John Evans's book, *Morals Not Knowledge*, raises the importance of ethics in the relationship between science and Christianity, especially in the United States. He summarizes "religion and science are the two great ways of understanding the world, but by understanding I mean the relationships between humans in the world and the relationship between humans and nature. These are stuff of morality."[43] Evans argues that it is here, at the crossroads of Christian morals that conflicts with science and particularly conservative Christianity. "Evolution versus creation," for example, isn't ultimately about doctrine, in this view, but about the implications for ethics.

Among other insights from her social scientific research, Ecklund has similarly highlighted that Christians are particularly drawn to sciences that involve healing—that is, ethical action in the world that reduces suffering. She observes that Christians and non-Christians both express "a great deal of confidence in medicine."[44] This correlates with a focus on Jesus, who is reported in the Gospels to be a healer. As Ecklund observes,

> Jesus's ministry on earth involved touching those whom others would not touch, healing those whom others thought were beyond healing. Christians holding this theological view can see medical technologies as created by God for us to use to relieve our suffering and the suffering of others.[45]

Given the length of this chapter, I'll have to take recourse in simply summarizing other key ethical issues. This indeed leads to ethical action simply not for other humans but for the Earth. As with evolution, even though there is clearly loud Christian resistance to admitting that human activity has caused global warming, almost all major representative of Christianity—notably Pope Francis and evangelical climate scientist Katherine Hayhoe—supports active creation care, which includes combatting climate change. And though Philip Clayton has highlighted stem cell research, warfare technology, CRISPR gene editing, he reserves particular attention for global climate and sets Christianity within the "three Abrahamic faiths [which] go back . . . to the Book of Genesis, which calls believers to cultivate care for the earth." Nature for them is "a creation of God and therefore a thing of great value."[46]

Final thoughts

This has been a longish chapter, and so I'll be brief here. "Simple, far too simple" is a worthy rejoinder to most slogans about religion and science, but especially about Christianity and science. It's a vast and diverse religious tradition, and its adherents are varied. Its history of interaction, including both successes and failures, cannot be overlooked. And at the same time, will history set the agenda for future viability? I can't help but conclude that Christianity will remain a fascinating and vital locus for the interaction of religion and science.

Suggestions for further reading

In this and the following chapters, I've limited myself to just a few key texts. You can find more resources, if interested, in the endnotes.

There is no lack of resources for this chapter. Here again, I'll recommend Alister McGrath, *Science and Religion: A New Introduction*, especially his 2nd ed. (Oxford: Basil-Blackwell, 2010). For a very user-friendly approach, see Elaine Howard Ecklund, *Why Science and Faith Need Each Other* (Grand Rapids, MI: Brazos, 2020). I've tried my own hand at this with a particular look at 18–30-year-olds, *Mere Science and Christian Faith: Bridging the Divide with Emerging Adults* (Downers Grove, IL: InterVarsity Press, 2018). On particular topics, I recommend the following: Gary Fugle, *Laying Down Arms to Heal the Creation-Evolution Divide* (Eugene, OR: Wipf & Stock, 2015), Ted Peters's three books, *Astrotheology: Science and Theology Meet Extraterrestrial Life* (Eugene, OR: Cascade, 2018), *God—The World's Future: Systematic Theology for a New Era*, 2nd ed. (Minneapolis, MN: Fortress, 2000), and *Playing God? Genetic Determinism and Human Freedom*, 2nd edition (New York: Routledge, 2002).

Notes

1 Francis Collins, interview in Steve Paulson, *Atoms and Eden: Conversations on Religion and Science* (Oxford: Oxford University Press, 2010), 31.
2 Ecklund and Scheitle, *Religion vs. Science: What Religious People Really Think* (Oxford: Oxford University Press, 2018), 3.

3 Stephen Prothero, *God Is Not One: The Eight Rival Religions That Run the World* (New York: HarperOne, 2010), 13–6.

4 Pew Research Center, "Scientists and Belief," www.pewforum.org/2009/11/05/scientists-and-belief, accessed 14 June 2022.

5 Baruch A. Shalev, *100 Years of Nobel Prizes* (Boston, MA: Atlantic Publishers & Distributors, 2003), 57.

6 Prothero, *God Is Not One*, 107.

7 Richard Dawkins, *The Selfish Gene*, 2nd ed. (Oxford: Oxford University Press, 1989), 198.

8 Mark Twain, *Huckleberry Finn*, www.goodreads.com/quotes/1187463-having-faith-is-believing-in-something-you-just-know-ain-t, accessed 14 June 2022.

9 Galileo, "Letter to Grand Duchess Christina of Tuscany," https://barelymore-thanatweet.com/2021/01/27/galileos-letter-to-grand-duchess-christina-of-tuscany, accessed 14 June 2022.

10 C.S. Lewis, *Mere Christianity* (New York: Macmillan, 1952), 123.

11 See Lawrence M. Principe, *The Scientific Revolution: A Very Short Introduction* (Oxford: Oxford University Press, 2011), which can be joined with the classic treatment by A.N. Whitehead, *Science and the Modern World* (New York: Macmillan, 1925); Noah Ephron's essay, "That Christianity Gave Birth to Modern Science," in *Galileo Goes to Jail and Other Myths about Science and Religion,* ed. Ron Numbers (Cambridge, MA: Harvard University Press, 2010).

12 Townes, *Science and Theology: The New Consonance*, ed. Ted Peters (Boulder, CO: Westview Press, 1998), 46.

13 David Masci, "For Darwin Day, 6 Facts about the Evolution Debate," www.pewresearch.org/fact-tank/2019/02/11/darwin-day, accessed 14 June 2022.

14 Charles Kingsley, "The Natural Theology of the Future," read at Sion College, 10 January 1871," www.online-literature.com/charles-kingsley/scientific/7, accessed 14 June 2022.

15 My four views are rough similar to, but not the same as, what is presented here: Matthew and Ardel B. Canedy, general eds., *Four Views on the Historical Adam* (Grand Rapids, MI: Zondervan, 2013).

16 "Evolutionary creation" is the preferred term of BioLogos, the nonprofit organization Collins started in 2009. See https://biologos.org.

17 Cootsona, *Mere Science and Christian Faith: Bridging the Divide With Emerging Adults* (Downers Grove, IL: InterVarsity Press, 2018), ch. 5.

18 Gary Fugle, *Laying Down Arms to Heal the Creation-Evolution Divide* (Eugene, OR: Wipf & Stock, 2015); Joshua Swamidass, *The Geneaological Adam and Eve* (Downers Grove, IL: InterVarsity Press, 2021).

19 C.S. Lewis, *Problem of Pain* (New York: Macmillan, 1962), 77. See also, David Venema and Scot McKnight, *Adam and the Genome: Reading Scripture after Genetics Science* (Grand Rapids, MI: Brazos, 2017).

20 See Beth Braxland, "Hominid and Hominin—What's the Difference?" http://australianmuseum.net.au/hominid-and-hominin-whats-the-difference, accessed 14 June 2022.

21 See my essay, "*Sensus Divinitatis*," in *Connecting Faith and Science: Philosophical and Theological Inquiries,* Claremont Studies in Science and Religion, vol. 1; Hill, Holtzen, eds. (Claremont, CA: Claremont Press, 2017).

22 Justin Barrett, *Born Believers: The Science of Children's Religious Belief* (New York: Atria, 2019); Pascal Boyer, *Religion Explained: The Evolutionary Origins of Religious Thought* (New York: Basic Books, 2002).

23 Barrett, *Cognitive Science, Religion, and Theology: From Human Minds to Divine Minds*, Templeton Science and Religion Series (West Conshohocken: Templeton Press, 2011).
24 Barrett, "Cognitive Science of Religion and Christian Faith: How May They Be Brought Together?" www.asa3.org/ASA/PSCF/2017/PSCF3-17Barrett.pdf, accessed 14 June 2022.
25 Barrett, *Cognitive Science*, 71.
26 Andrew Newberg and Eugene D'Aquili, *Why God Won't Go Away: Brain Science and the Biology of Belief* (New York: Ballantine Books, 2002).
27 McCauley, *Why Religion Is Natural and Science Is Not* (Oxford: Oxford University Press, 2011).
28 Cited in Timothy Ferris, *Coming of Age in the Milky Way* (New York: HarperCollins, 2003), 211.
29 Hoyle, *Facts and Dogmas in Cosmology and Elsewhere* (Cambridge: Cambridge University Press, 1982), 2f.; cited in Southgate et al., 36.
30 Krauss, *A Universe from Nothing: Why There Is Something Rather Than Nothing* (New York: Atria Books, 2013).
31 Jastrow, *God and the Astronomers* (New York: Norton, 1992), 125.
32 McGrath, *Science and Religion: A New Introduction*, 2nd ed. (Oxford: Wiley-Blackwell, 2010), 152.
33 "Fine-Tuned Universe," https://en.wikipedia.org/wiki/Fine-tuned_Universe, accessed 14 June 2022.
34 Note John Polkinghorne's concerns about the term, "Anthropic Principle," in *Science and Religion in Quest of Truth* (New Haven, CT and London: Yale University, 2011), 54–5.
35 Freeman Dyson, *Disturbing the Universe* (New York: Harper & Row, 1979), 256.
36 Gingrich, *God's Planet* (Cambridge, MA: Harvard University Press, 2015).
37 McGrath, *Science and Religion*, 155.
38 "Exoplanet Exploration," https://exoplanets.nasa.gov, accessed 14 June 2022.
39 Jeff Schweitzer, "Earth 2.0: Bad News for God," www.huffpost.com/entry/earth-20-bad-news-for-god_b_7861528?guccounter=1, accessed 14 June 2022.
40 *Counterbalance*, https://counterbalance.org/etsurv/index-frame.html, accessed 14 June 2022.
41 See C.S. Lewis, "Religion and Rocketry," www.cslewis.com/religion-and-rocketry, accessed 14 June 2022.
42 Ted Peters, *Astrotheology: Science and Theology Meet Extraterrestrial Life* (Eugene, OR: Cascade, 2018).
43 Evans, *Morals Not Knowledge: Recasting the Contemporary U.S. Conflict between Religion and Science* (Berkeley, CA: University of California Press, 2018), 171.
44 The actual percentages are 35% and 38%, respectively. See Elaine Howard Ecklund, *Why Science and Faith Need Each Other* (Grand Rapids, MI: Brazos, 2020), 113.
45 Ibid., 114.
46 Clayton, *Religion and Science: The Basics* (Oxfordshire: Routledge), 184.

3 Streaming science and spirituality
The Spiritual but Not Religious

In the process of writing this book, I regularly passed by my parents' wedding picture. My mother is attired in an elegant satin ivory dress and my father is in a chic double-breasted white tuxedo jacket. Stunning in their 1940s attire, their beautiful, young smiling faces clearly express a radiant happiness as they walk down the steps just after they've been declared "husband and wife." But one element of the photograph particularly caught my attention. Right above their heads—though they were not particularly religious—is a clear indication of the setting, "First Methodist Church."

In a way, this shouldn't surprise me. In their day, it was assumed that you were married in a church and that you were Christian. That day, however, is past. Religious affiliation no longer represents the default mode for Americans. And one group is part of this change, transforming not just religion but also the interaction of religion and science and what that interaction means.

In this chapter, I consider a group of Americans that reject the term "religious," though there remains something worth pursuing at the core of religious life. They call themselves—or at least, are called by others—"Spiritual but Not Religious" (SBNR). To quote an insight attributed to Father Patrick Collins, "Religion is for those who are afraid of going to hell. Spirituality is for those who know they have been there—perhaps through involvement with religion."[1]

SBNR is the fastest growing religious group in our country, and it has also emerged as the second largest. Christians used to represent 95% of the US population in 1960, and it has dropped from 75% to 63% between 2007 and 2021.[2] While other religions remained largely unchanged, those not affiliating with any one tradition (which, of course, includes SBNR) jumped from 16% to 29%. The market share lost by Christianity in the past decade or so has not been taken up by other religions, but almost entirely by SBNR.

"Whether we believe in God or not, I think most of us have a sense of the spiritual, that recognition of a deeper meaning and purpose in our lives, and I believe that this sense flourishes despite the pressures of our

DOI: 10.4324/9781003214236-3

world." Maybe it shouldn't have surprised me that Queen Elizabeth II pronounced this on her 2000 Christmas Day Broadcast.[3] In the United Kingdom, those with no religious affiliation have overtaken those identifying as Christian. And to many in the United States, Spiritual but Not Religious sounds like something very recent. And yet, it first appeared as a term in 1926, when the Rotary Club president declared his group as "inclusive, nonsectarian, and notably, as Spiritual but Not Religious."[4] Alcoholics Anonymous (AA) is often credited with subsequently spreading this distinct use of "spiritual" as opposed to "religious." In fact, AA meetings have remained venues where spirituality continues to flourish in our country.

At any rate, the differentiation of spiritual from religious has become part of our contemporary lexicon.

Introducing SBNRs: another lightning round Q & A

Here is a brief introduction to a key religious demographic that wouldn't be very comfortable with the label of being a "religious."

Is there any one particular characteristic that defines SBNRs?

Most SBNRs have a strong distaste or dislike for religious institutions. These are people who find a deep spiritual connection with the world around them and seek transcendence beyond the material world and have a particularly high propensity psychologically to be open to new experiences.

Can you say more about the phrase, "Spiritual but Not Religious"?

Two scholars writing about this group, Linda Woodhead and Paul Heelas, set out this distinction,

> Most notably the term "spirituality" is often used to express commitment to a deep truth that is to be found within what belongs to this world. And the term "religion" is used to express commitment to a higher truth that is "out there," lying beyond what this world has to offer, and *exclusively* related to specific externals (scriptures, dogmas, rituals, and so on).[5]

I italicized *exclusively* because this is key to SBNR: the exclusivism of religion is one critical reason to reject it.

Put another way, what then is the problem and what is the solution that SBNR presents?

The problem is that religions are inadequate means to express and live out spirituality, and so we must set out a new course, which is attuned to our individual, or perhaps community, needs, and commitments.

How many are in the SBNR demographic?

I turn to Fuller and Parsons, "A judicious synthesis of existing research indicates that somewhere between 18% to 27% of the U.S. population can be considered SBNR as opposed to being either traditionally religious or wholly nonreligious."[6] They also skew toward the emerging adult, or 18–30-year-old, demographic.

How do the "Spiritual but Not Religious" (SBNR) relate to the nones?

When asked "What religious affiliation are you?" they check the box "none of the above," and thus, the name "nones." Many people therefore are both none and SBNR. On a related note, there are some precedents to SBNR under the name, "New Age," but the use of that particular term has faded in the past decade or so.

What are the forms this can take?

Here, I would include religious naturalism in addition to the more standard none and "done" (once involved in a more formal religion, but no longer are), pantheists, and even "spiritual atheist scientists." Woodhead and Heelas set out this list[7]:

> the multifarious forms of sacred activity which are often grouped together under collective terms like "body, mind and spirit," "New Age," "alternative" or "holistic" spirituality, and which include (spiritual) yoga, reiki, meditation, tai chi, aromatherapy, much paganism, rebirthing, reflexology, much wicca and many more.

(As you can see, this overlaps with my chapter on nature religions.)

Are there any notable leaders?

Some examples are Alan Watts and Ram Das in the past; Eckhart Tolle, Deepak Chopra, and Oprah Winfrey today.

Discussing SBNRs and science with Elaine Howard Ecklund

To assist me on this journey, I've interviewed a preeminent sociologist of religion and science, Dr. Elaine Howard Ecklund of Rice University, to be sure that I take in the full picture (or at least as much as I can do in this brief chapter). When I think of Ecklund's work, she brings striking intellectual acumen to social scientific research. She has authored several books—the most relevant are *Science vs. Religion*, *Religion vs. Science*, *Secularity and Science*—as well as numerous research articles. In writing this,

I also can't help but recall her laugh and her sense of humor, even as I contemplate that this is also the scholar who delivered the prestigious Gifford Lectures in 2019. To be sure, her influence travels far beyond Rice—her work has appeared in *Time, BBC, Scientific American, The Chronicle of Higher Education, The Washington Post,* and *CNN.com.* And that's not all, but it's enough to underline that she and her work are impressive.

I asked about what frames her work as a sociologist, "Thinking about different kinds of social identities and social groups and how they interface with one another and have an impact on both religion and science and the relationship between religion and science."[8]

Indeed, to grasp the SBNR demographic, you have to get the sociological dimension right. Part of our discussion centered around the sociology of religion in America. We talked about the book she co-authored with David R. Johnson, which is critically important for grasping this demographic and how they relate to science, *Varieties of Atheism in Science.*[9] They particularly highlight "Spiritual Atheists Scientists" (where "atheist scientist" represents a key designation for their work). So, it might sound odd, but we can't leave out atheists entirely in this category. Ecklund and Johnson have found that there are 22% of scientific atheists who were interested in spirituality. They comment, "The nascent literature on scientists' spirituality suggests that scientists might perceive being SBNR as an innovative way to even navigate tensions between science and religion."[10]

How SBNR came to be

As I mentioned in the Introduction, the form of each chapter follows the function of its content. In this case, understanding SBNRs, and their history, is a necessary step and will take a larger portion of this chapter than most in this book.

Varying from the institutional norm of religion is not particularly new, and it is deeply American. The Transcendentalist thinker Ralph Waldo Emerson, in his famous 1838 speech at Harvard Divinity School, treads this path. Consider the way he reinvents Jesus. And if the language were updated a bit, Emerson would sound strikingly contemporary:

> And thus by his holy thoughts, Jesus serves us, and thus only. To aim to convert a man by miracles, is a profanation of the soul. A true conversion, a true Christ, is now, as always, to be made, by the reception of beautiful sentiments.[11]

Early, in his journals, Emerson tied the spiritual quest with embracing or rejecting science. "The religion that is afraid of science dishonors God and commits suicide. Every influx of atheism, of skepticism, is thus made useful as a mercury pill assaulting and removing a diseased religion, and making way for truth."[12]

Research and interviews demonstrate that SBNRs are generally averse to religious institutions,[13] and they are often specifically opposed to Christianity and its exclusivism. Two key spiritual practices for SBNRs are mindfulness meditation and "spending time in nature for reflection."[14] If they are drawn to any of the traditions in this book, it is either Buddhist modernism or nature religions.

Here is an appropriate place to add that, for scholars of religion, the terms *spirituality* and *religion*, however, can be reasonably coterminous. Influential scholar Huston Smith's famous summary of religion, "a way of life woven around a people's ultimate concerns,"[15] makes them sound almost indistinguishable. Or as professor of religion Robert Fuller puts it summarily in discussing the designation SBNR, "The words *spiritual* and *religious* have historically been synonymous."[16]

For SBNRs, the key problem is that religions seek to unilaterally control ideas and behaviors, and that critical oxygen for spirituality is an amalgam of religious ideas. Or as Leigh Eric Schmidt begins his book *Restless Souls*, " 'One day I woke up and wondered: maybe today I should be a Christian, or would I rather be a Buddhist, or am I just a *Star Trek* freak?' So one woman told a sociologist who studies contemporary American religion."[17]

The connection with emerging adulthood

SBNRs skew younger toward emerging adults (age 18–30). As I've argued elsewhere,[18] a rising, new form of pluralism seems to be the future. Emerging adults tend to create a streaming spirituality mix rather than a monolithic LP religion (a topic I'll address in a subsequent section). In an interview with Zoe, age 20, I heard this: "I don't ever think of myself as a religious person. However, I prefer taking pieces of some different religions."

My own qualitative interviews clearly support the conclusion that we are turning into a nation with more SBNRs and fewer Christians. In fact, I am drawing on interviews with 43 emerging adults and surveys of 18- to 30-year-olds from an 18-month research grant project for which I served as principal investigator, Science for Students and Emerging, Young Adults (SEYA).[19] This project analyzed emerging adult attitudes of 18–30-year-olds on faith and science, specifically how they are formed and change. In brief, the SEYA team taught the integration of science and religion with emerging adult participants and had informal discussions about how they related science and religion.

We presented target groups in Northern California and New York City with a questionnaire based on surveys from leading researchers, Christian Smith,[20] as well as David Kinnaman and Aly Hawkin.[21] During a period of 4 to 6 weeks, these groups read and discussed resources such as Alister McGrath's *Science and Religion: A New Introduction*[22] or the DVD *Test of Faith* (developed by the Faraday Institute at Cambridge University[23]). Our team surveyed these emerging adults before and after to draw conclusions on how they see science and religion and how science affects spirituality. I've supplemented these results with my interviews.

Because SBNRs and 18–30-year-olds are so deeply connected, my portrait here emphasizes emerging adults. Consequently, it draws less on, for example, the Burning Man Festival—a key yearly event with about 46% identifying as SBNR[24]—whose median age is 35.[25] And since I've employed the *emerging adult*, I need to define it. First of all, why not just "adult"? In 2000, Jeffery Arnett developed the category of "emerging adulthood"[26] as a stage of life that is no longer adolescence but between adolescence and full adulthood. Let it be said that I am not committed to all the implications of this designation.[27] (For one thing, many in low socio-economic conditions are forced to develop job skills early and often move into adult responsibilities more quickly.[28])

Nevertheless, the reasons for developing this sociological category are reasonably evident. Previously, five milestones defined adulthood, at least as a sociological category: "leaving home, finishing school, becoming financially independent, getting married, and having children."[29] But the age at which these milestones are reached has shifted later.[30] In his study of this demographic, Princeton University sociologist Robert Wuthnow focused on two markers: Americans are marrying and having children later.[31] Research on Gen Z (born in 1996) indicates that, by age 30, only one in four intend to marry and one in six plan to have children.[32]

This has some particular outcomes. With a longer period to emerge into adulthood, 18–30-year-olds often display five interrelated characteristics: (1) they seek personal meaning and identity; (2) their lives are marked instability through regular job relocations, moves, and revision of life plans; (3) they tend to be self-focused, liberated from parental oversight and significant responsibility for others; (4) they feel "in between"—beyond adolescent life but not yet at full adult status; and (5) emerging adults exist in an "age of possibilities," optimistic about the future and keeping their options open.[33] Arnett's conclusion offers an illuminating perspective on what emerging adults are bringing to the study of science and religion: "Having left the dependency of childhood and adolescence, and having not yet entered the enduring responsibilities that are normative to adulthood, emerging adults often explore a variety of possible life directions in love, work, and worldviews."[34] These worldviews naturally include both scientific and religious, or spiritual, inputs.

And all of these forces turbocharge the movement away from religious institutions and toward a broader "streaming spirituality."

How technology formed SBNR spirituality

Technology and science may be shaped by religion—as is the case with nature religions and their deep connection with environmental sustainability, or the rise of modern science in countries with monotheistic religions. In America, however, more often science leaves its indelible imprint on religious movements, and particularly here with SBNR. The relationship between SBNR and technology is a symbiosis. In a conversation in my Science and Religion course, when I asked how to integrate science and spirituality, one student answered, "Science puts spirituality into action. In many ways, science intentionally moves us into areas we don't yet know. And that's very spiritual."

Put another way, a key driving force for SBNR approach is the growth of technology, not as some kind of metaphor but as a mover of culture and psychology. This is particularly the case for emerging adults, who grew up as digital natives, that is, in environments saturated with options available to them almost ubiquitously through smartphones. The array of knowledge on the internet—with the number of websites over one billion—intensifies the array of potential spiritual inputs and presents thought leaders besides then neighborhood imams, priests, pastors, and rabbis. This shift in authority does not stand alone. I'm already mentioned various interviews and conversations with emerging adults. There I've heard this numerous times, "my parents didn't want me to grow up with any one religion, and so they let me choose."

It also relates to the shift in online dating culture. Some commentators note that the term SBNR took a perceptible uptick demographically when online dating first became popular in the early 2000s. Matthew Hedstrom, a professor of religion at the University of Virginia as commented about dating apps,

> You had to identify by religion, you had to check a box. . . . Spiritual-but-not-religious' became a nice category that said, "I'm not some kind of cold-hearted atheist, but I'm not some kind of moralizing, prudish person, either. I'm nice, friendly, and spiritual—but not religious."[35]

And so too, major polling and research organizations began to add this category.

Streaming life, science, and spirituality

All of this adds up to what I've labeled "streaming spirituality," and thus "streaming science and religion." No longer is religious belief a vinyl 12-inch LP where you start with side A first, then side B. Even more, *the LP almost always has one band who set the song sequence.* By analogy, do we take the Catechism of the Catholic Church, play it all the way through, and then decide to believe the whole shebang or not? That's not what I'm reading or hearing. Today, the sequence set by the musical or ecclesiastical authorities neither directs nor constrains decisions about spirituality or religious affiliation.

Emerging adults arrange a bricolage of religious inputs, and this creates streaming spirituality (or maybe alternatively, "Spotify spirituality"). In my college classes, students tell me clearly, "No religion can tell me what to wear or what to believe or whom to love." Seekers instead assemble a variety of spiritual inputs. By using a mix, listeners create a playlist from various artists based on a feel or a mood. "I like listening to Kendrick Lamar, but why not throw in some John Coltrane?" They seek to create something new and individualized. Or at least that's what it seems to us. But here's an irony that technology creates—we rarely actually curate this mix; instead, we often outsource it to a curating algorithm assembled by able computer programmers whether it's in music or our spiritual life.

In a similar vein, Wuthnow described the lifestyle of many 18–30-year-olds as *bricoleurs* or "tinkerers" who assemble of variety of disparate objects to create a composite. "A tinkerer puts together a life from whatever skills, ideas, and resources that are readily at hand."[36] Therefore, they often become what he dubs " 'spiritual bricoleurs,' by piecing together ideas about spirituality from many sources."[37]

Tinkering/bricolage/streaming all represent tactics for realizing one's personal spiritual expression—conversely it may also be one strategy for keeping a religious tradition viable. In my undergraduate Science and Religion class, one student with a background in the evangelical church commented, "I cherry pick from various religions instead of choosing just one." Another student added, "Ya, I'll stay with being a Catholic, but at times I like Buddhism better. So, I'll also go with that." As one student, Taylor, commented, "If someone is Catholic, they may not believe the whole. The way they stay in church is to pick and choose."

In sum, technology shapes spirituality.

Good ole American individualism

That characteristically American trait, *individualism*,[38] provides a root for this religious pluralism. In the nineteenth century, author and clergyman John Weiss offered this declaration: "America is an opportunity to make a Religion out of sacredness of the individual."[39]

Is the SBNR movement ultimately just an individualist's spiritual quest? Ecklund and I discussed the individualism that's an indelible and ongoing factor of American religious life.

> Some scholars may think of that "Spiritual but Not Religious" category in the U. S. as an extreme form of individualism. But it may also be deeply Christian and particularly Protestant. It may be somewhat of a "just me and God," often unmoored from tradition. But is the Spiritual but Not Religious movement actually able to move forward exactly because some of this movement—in the US at least—may actually have roots in our Protestant traditions? We're always living and breathing within traditions, whether we like it or not.

Some sociologists of religion in fact think this may be a place where "people are trying to put the individual above the community and then pick and choose from different kinds of community practices to make something which is distinctive."

This individualism "may have to stand against institutionalized religion to continue." It may need to describe the perspective of SNBRs (as Ecklund did):

> I'm not part of institutional religion necessarily, but I do want to have a deep and committed spirituality that's beyond the self that might reflectively draw from various religious traditions to refashion something that's really taking the best of those traditions to give me a framework for living more ethically in the world.

Emerging adults are certainly ratcheting up the machine of cultural change via American individualism—and withdrawing from formal or informal affiliation with religion, but I do not want to overstate this trend as purely a phenomenon of the young. Because of course it's not. All ages swim in the pool of American religious pluralism. Carol Lee Flinders (born in 1943) once remarked, "I cannot describe my spiritual practice as Buddhist . . . or as Hindu or Catholic or Sufi, though I feel that in a sense it is all of these."[40] Decades ago, a 1978 Gallup poll "found that 80% of Americans agreed that 'an individual should arrive at his or her religious beliefs independent of any churches or synagogues.'"[41] The final resting place of this individual choice creates a proliferating pluralism.

Scholars of contemporary religion offer a wider, historical view. This increasing individualist culture has resulted from gradual change, as Andrew Delbanco expertly described it: first, the locus of our hope as the basis for the American Dream was in God (the Puritans); then, in Nation; and since the 1960s, in Self.[42] His meditation on "the real American Dream" concluded with this, "Today, hope has narrowed to the vanishing point of the self alone."[43] Historians of American religion Edwin Gaustad and Leigh Schmidt add, "America's vast religious marketplace—its cornucopia of therapies, advice books, spiritual techniques, retreat centers, angels, Christian diets, and small groups—now shapes religious identities in its own multiplicitous and ever-shifting image."[44]

Ethics are not peripheral

All of this could be about SBNR ethics. In this view, the searching for spirituality, without affiliating with any particular religious institution, is not simply about knowledge, but also about ethics. I've mentioned previously John Evans, but his work comes to mind as does the writings of Jonathan Haidt,[45] of how this search can be formed and driven by "intuitive cognitions" or "feelings of certainty."[46] Despite their unwillingness to be boxed into institutions, SBNR rejection of any particular scientific conclusions often overrides rational concerns because those in "my tribe" don't subscribe. For example, Ecklund reminded me that the nones are a group that often is anti-vaccination.

Venues are shifting, and emerging adults arrive at their conclusions in new ways. When seeking truths about science outside of religious communities, 18–30-year-olds—and increasingly Americans in general—are often distrustful of the church, synagogue, or mosque as a place to seek out answers about science and religion. One of the key convictions is that SBNRs often find it immoral to continue to subscribe to a particular religion—which is generally in the United States, Christianity—when it is seen as exclusive, homophobic, politically reactionary, racist, etc. And frequently science, popularly presented, provides support. As Taylor told me in an interview, it's "proven in science that you don't choose to be gay. Denying that makes you look ignorant."

In 1985, the authors of *Habits of Heart* found this in *Sheilaism*. "I believe in God. I'm not a religious fanatic. I can't remember the last time I went to church. My faith has carried me a long way. It's Sheilaism.

Just my own little voice."[47] To cite *Wikipedia*, Sheilaism represents "a shorthand term for an individual's system of religious belief which co-opts strands of multiple religions chosen by the individual usually without much theological consideration."[48] For SBNRs, Sheilaism can be a strategy for practicing selected portions of a religion that doesn't affirm one's sexual identity, as scholar Melissa Wilcox has argued in "When Sheila's a Lesbian."[49] More broadly, this could be a radical commitment to retain the goods of a religious tradition without rejecting a wholesale. It can also be a way to admit that none of us live fully within the confines or commands of a religion, but we may want to draw from it nonetheless.

Since churches and other religious institutions are ethically suspect, SBNRs are a key part of expanding those who curate the conversation between science and religion. In the past, we could assume that people discuss science and religion in congregations, and in academic institutions such as seminaries, Christian colleges, and sometimes, public universities. But this is shifting. When I asked my emerging adults where they would go to find out answers about science and/or religion, the most common answer was "the internet" or "Google."

As an ethical stance, SBNRs are more supportive of the efforts to combat climate change than the United States as a whole. The Pew Report found that about two-thirds of the religious unaffiliated see that climate change is human-caused. And it added, "When it comes to people's beliefs about climate change, it is the religiously unaffiliated, not those who identify with a religious tradition, who are particularly likely to say the Earth is warming due to human activity."[50]

On technology, SBNR, and transhumanism

Technology and the SBNR movement indeed exist in symbiosis. Here, I'll add two other connections. SBNRs find spirituality through popular media and gaming and can adapt their rituals easily to online spaces. Scholar of religion Sarah Pike has demonstrated the ease at which the famous Burning Man Festival in Black Rock, Nevada, moved into a virtual space during the early years of the COVID-19 pandemic.[51]

Similarly, SBNRs also often subscribe to transhumanism or posthumanism and the ability of technology to help human beings transcend the limitations of biologically based life. Interestingly, I learned that *transhuman* is actually quite old. Meghan O'Gieblyn, in writing about her rejection of evangelical Christianity and her steps into transhumanism, finds this—which I quote to demonstrate that the spiritual urge to transcend our boundaries has long roots:

> The word transhuman first appeared not in a work of science or technology but in Henry Francis Carey's 1814 translation of Dante's *Paradiso*, the final book of the *Divine Comedy*. Dante has completed his journey through paradise and is ascending into the spheres of heaven when his human flesh is suddenly transformed. He is vague about the nature of his new body. "Words may not tell of that transhuman change," he writes.

She sees transhumanists as taking up then some very old traditions while using modern technology to rework them and often to cast off God. But she warns that this sometimes draws the same baggage of Christian eschatology that transhumanists seek to shed.

Most SBNRs embrace transhumanism's goals nonetheless. SBNRs seek and find that technology offers transcendence. And thus, as Albert R. Antosca wrote for *Slate* magazine, "Transhumanism is disrupting the debate on science and religion by showing us a new way of framing the issue."[52] It is often a way to seek spiritually without recourse to the goal of finding God, but almost god-like human beings.

Approaching science and religion as an SBNR

The cultural tradition in the United States of religious pluralism, picking and choosing among various inputs for spirituality, is venerable. I've just discussed the refashioning of religion that's a part of SBNR life. This also has a substantial impact on what spirituality or religion we bring to science and of how science is understood. Science is not ultimately an individual practice. Water boils at 100 degree Celsius for me or for my wife or my friends, despite our individual preferences.

And so, I asked Ecklund, "What does that mean for science and religion and the science or religion relationship?"[53]

First of all, we discussed her work on

> scientists who are spiritual but not religious. They just think of themselves as being more ethical than atheistic scientists. They think of themselves as being better mentors. They see themselves living for something beyond the self and having more of a communitarian spirit and being more reflective about their impact on the world and their vision for how their scientific work has an impact in the world.

Second, Ecklund told me that, partly through the characteristic American individualism, people are

> reforming and refashioning institutional religion. And there are also the Spiritual but Not Religious who are reforming and refashioning science, and what kinds of implications science might have for the world. They're not accepting institutional forms of religion, but they're not accepting institutional forms of science either. For example, you have considerable vaccine resistance in among some groups of Spiritual but Not Religious.

The relationship between science and technology is not whole-hearted embrace. One key component of SBNR is the resistance to scientism or scientific naturalism—that the material world is all that exists. Put bluntly, SBNRs may learn from Jerry Coyne and Richard Dawkins, but they reject their hard-edged atheism. Instead, they find there is more, even—if I may use capitalization—*Something* that transcends this world.

My own research has led me to the conclusion that young adults— who skew today's SBNR—have refashioned collaboration or integration of science with religion/spirituality.[54] They often see a conflict at the popular level but seek something else personally and individually. And since individuality represents a core component of SBNR spirituality, I'm willing to conclude that they are part of an emerging trend, which they are simultaneously intensifying. Work in religion and science can learn from SBNRs since this movement presents ways to transcend a simplistic warfare or conflict thesis, presenting instead a generative and integrative model.

Certainly not scriptural literalists

As I've mentioned, I've focused a considerable amount here on the formation and expansion of SBNRs in our country, and so I will be briefer with beliefs. Leading SBNR scholar Linda Mercadante has been particularly emphatic that SBNRs don't simply reject institutional religious ideas, they also promote various beliefs.[55] Yes, SBNRs do say things like "I'm a Druid-Celtic-Native American-Judeo-Christian" as a rejection of religious exclusivism. They also affirm a transcendence "there is a sacred dimension that is larger than your self," the goodness of human nature (and thus a rejection of "sin," as they understand it), a community "that supported them and their growth, one where everyone was free to believe and practice as they wished, and one that didn't make too many demands," and generally believe in reincarnation as a form of ongoing individual progress through subsequent lives.[56]

SBNRs tend to love books and videos. TED talks, events (like Burning Man), and popular speakers on YouTube—because they can be consumed individually—proliferate. Thus, there may even be key "scriptures" from these thought leaders—Deepak Chopra, Elizabeth Gilbert, *The Secret*, Eckert Tolle, and a few decade ago, M. Scott Peck's *The Road Less Traveled*. But given the SBNR ethos, there's progress, and so no scripture is definitive and final. All books and videos are provisional.

By definition—and this statement borders on the painfully obvious—even if SBNRs are inspired by a particular religion, they will always interpret a sacred text metaphorically when it contradicts science. This implies the model of independence coexistence for science and religion in a specific way. As Ecklund and Di write,

> By saying that science and religion do not conflict if people interpret religious texts on their own rather than accept their narratives as literal truth, SBNR scientists imply that people should detach the scientific connotations from religion. According to them, religions answers broader questions about life and its meaning but does not provide scientific explanations about our world.[57]

When this independence and separation is breached, this leads to the disdain I have often heard from SBNRs for biblical literalists who hold to their texts in a way that leads them to assert vehemently that the world was created a few thousand years ago in six 24-hour days. In the SBNR ethos, all texts are open to revision and even being supplanted.

Final thoughts

As the fastest growing US religious demographic, the Spiritual but Not Religious will continue to affect the relationship between science and religion—or perhaps better, science, and spirituality. The biggest challenge for SBNRs is whether they will be able to coalesce and create a effective movement. They do join together around issues and events, but in creating ongoing change, they are much less potent than their similarly sized counterpart, Christian political conservatives.

At the same time, we should not underestimate their influence and their contribution to science and religion, particularly in reducing the warfare thesis. As Ecklund and Di write, "SBNR scientists are sometimes seen as ambassadors bridging the cultural and ideological divide between science and religion. Indeed, as reflected in our survey results, being spiritual cushions 'the conflict narrative' between science and religion in most national/social contexts."[58] And thus SBRNs might indeed be the leaders of new paradigms, the kind really, that change the way a book like this can be written. (But be assured: I will forge ahead nevertheless.)

Suggestions for further reading

To grasp SBNRs, a perfect starting place is the collection of essays edited by William B. Parsons, *Being Spiritual But Not Religious: Past, Present, Future(s)* (New York: Routledge, 2018), and Paul Heelas and Linda Woodhead, *The Spiritual Revolution: Why Religion Is Giving Way to Spirituality* (Oxford: Blackwell, 2005). For a history of American religious history to set the context, check out Leigh Eric Schmidt, *Restless Souls: The Making of American Spirituality* (New York: HarperCollins Publishers, 2005). These two texts connect this movement specifically with science: Elaine Howard Ecklund and David R. Johnson, *Varieties of Atheism in Science* (Oxford: Oxford University Press, 2021), and Elaine Howard Ecklund, *Science vs. Religion: What Scientists Really Think* (Oxford: Oxford University Press, 2010).

It is critical to appreciate the link between SBNR and emerging adults (18–30-year-olds). These texts are all good for understanding the latter demographic: Jonathan Hill, *Emerging Adulthood and Faith* (Grand Rapids, MI: Calvin College Press, 2015); Christian Smith with Patricia Snell, *Souls in Transition: The Religious and Spiritual Lives of Emerging Adults* (Oxford: Oxford University Press, 2009), and Robert Wuthnow, *After the Baby Boomers How Twenty- and Thirty-Somethings Are Shaping the Future of American Religion* (Princeton, NJ: Princeton University Press, 2007).

Notes

1 See https://quotepark.com/quotes/2087624-vine-deloria-jr-religion-is-for-people-whore-afraid-of-going-to-h, accessed 18 September 2022, citing Father Patrick Collins, *Awakened India* 99 (1994): 327.
2 Pew Research Center, "About Three-in-Ten U.S. Adults Are Now Religiously Unaffiliated," https://www.pewresearch.org/religion/2021/12/14/about-three-in-ten-u-s-adults-are-now-religiously-unaffiliated, accessed 17 September 2022.
3 See https://gainfordwinston.church/queen-elizabeth-ii-the-servant-queen, accessed 15 June 2022.
4 *The American Mercury*, 9 October 1926; in William B. Parsons, ed., *Being Spiritual But Not Religious: Past, Present, Future(s)* Routledge Studies in Religion (New York and London: Routledge, 2018).
5 Paul Heelas and Linda Woodhead, *The Spiritual Revolution: Why Religion Is Giving Way to Spirituality* (Oxford: Blackwell, 2005), 6.

6 Fuller and Parsons, in ed. William B. Parsons, *Being Spiritual But Not Religious: Past, Present, Future(s)*, 27. See also Michael Lipka and Claire Gecewicz, "More Americans Now Say They're Spiritual But Not Religious," 6 September 2017, www.pewresearch.org/fact-tank/2017/09/06/more-americans-now-say-theyre-spiritual-but-not-religious, accessed 15 June 2022.

7 Heelas and Woodhead, *The Spiritual Revolution*. p 7.

8 Private conversation, recorded on 15 July 2021.

9 Elaine Howard Ecklund and David R. Johnson, *Varieties of Atheism in Science* (Oxford: Oxford University Press, 2021), especially 76–93.

10 Ecklund and Johnson, *Varieties of Atheism in Science*, 80–1.

11 Emerson, https://emersoncentral.com/texts/nature-addresses-lectures/addresses/divinity-school-address, accessed 16 May 2022.

12 Journals of Ralph Waldo Emerson, 4 March 1831, quoted in *The Journals and Miscellaneous Notebooks of Ralph Waldo Emerson* (Cambridge, MA: Harvard University Press, 1963), 239.

13 Fuller article, "Minds of Their Own," in *Being Spiritual But Not Religious*, ed. Parsons, 89ff.

14 Robert C. Fuller, *Spiritual, But Not Religious: Understanding Unchurched America* (Oxford: Oxford University Press, 2001), 76–100; Barna Group, "Meet the 'Spiritual But Not Religious'," www.barna.com/research/meet-spiritual-not-religious/, accessed 20 May 2022.

15 Huston Smith, *The World's Religions* (New York: Harper SanFrancisco, 1991), 183.

16 Fuller, "Minds of Their Own," 90.

17 Leigh Eric Schmidt, *Restless Souls: The Making of American Spirituality* (Berkeley, CA: University of California Press, 2012), 1.

18 Greg Cootsona, "Some Ways Emerging Adults Are Shaping the Future of Science and Religion," *Zygon: Journal of Religion and Science* 51, no. 3 (2016): 557–72. See also Robert Wuthnow, *After the Baby Boomers: How Twenty- and Thirty-Somethings Are Shaping the Future of American Religion* (Princeton, NJ, and Oxford: Princeton University Press, 2007), 14; cf. Melissa M. Wilcox, "When Sheila's a Lesbian: Religious Individualism among Lesbian, Gay, Bisexual, and Transgender Christians," *Sociology of Religion* 63, no. 4 (2002): 498.

19 www.templeton.org/grant/science-for-students-and-emerging-young-adults-seya, accessed 16 June 2022.

20 Christian Smith with Patricia Snell, *Souls in Transition: The Religious and Spiritual Lives of Emerging Adults* (Oxford: Oxford University Press, 2009).

21 David Kinnaman with Aly Hawkins, *You Lost Me: Why Young Christians Are Leaving Church . . . and Rethinking Faith* (Grand Rapids, MI: Baker Books, 2011).

22 Alister McGrath, *Religion and Science: A New Introduction*, 2nd ed. (Oxford: Wiley-Blackwell, 2010).

23 For more info, see Test of Faith, www.testoffaith.com, accessed 25 June 2019.

24 Sarah M. Pike, "Sarah Pike on Burning Man," 10 January 2022, CORH podcast, https://app.podcastguru.io/podcast/corh-values-1541228611/episode/season-3-3-sarah-pike-on-burning-man-9e8067a830ec3067b712baea4b0e8900, accessed 15 June 2022.

25 See SFIST, "Black Rock Census Shows Typical Burner Is White, Rich, Male," https://sfist.com/2019/07/30/black-rock-census-shows-typical-burning-man-attendee-is-white-rich-male, accessed 19 May 2022. See also Sarah Pike, "Do Avatars Weep? Ritual and Sacred Space at Virtual Burning Man," www.

tandfonline.com/doi/abs/10.1080/0048721X.2022.2051801, accessed 15 June 2022.

26 Jeffrey Arnett, "Emerging Adulthood: A Theory of Development From the Late Teens Through the Twenties," *American Psychologist* 55, no. 5 (2000): 469–80.

27 Jeffrey Arnett, Marion Klepp, Leo B. Hendry, and Jennifer L. Tanner, *Debating Emerging Adulthood: Stage or Process?* (New York: Oxford University Press, 2011).

28 David P. Setran and Chris A. Kiesling, *Spiritual Formation in Emerging Adulthood: A Practical Theology for College and Young Adult Ministry* (Grand Rapids, MI: Baker Books, 2013), 242, n. 12.

29 Ibid., 2.

30 "Five Markers of Adulthood Millennials Have Had to Give Up On," *The Guardian*, www.theguardian.com/lifeandstyle/2016/mar/10/five-markers-of-adulthood-millenials-have-had-to-give-up-on, accessed 13 June 2019.

31 Wuthnow, 11.

32 Barna Group, *Gen Z: The Culture, Beliefs and Motivations Shaping the Next Generation* (Ventura, CA: Barna Group, 2018), 32.

33 Arnett, "Emerging Adulthood"; summarized by Setran and Kiesling, 3–4.

34 Arnett, "Emerging Adulthood," 469.

35 Caroline Kitchener, "What It Means to Be Spiritual But Not Religious," *The Atlantic*, 11 January 2018.

36 Wuthnow, 13.

37 Ibid., 135.

38 Cf. Greg Cootsona, *Negotiating Science and Religion in America* (New York: Routledge, 2020), ch. 10.

39 John Weiss, *American Religion* (Boston, MA: Roberts Brothers, 1871), 47.

40 Cited in Edwin Gaustad and Leigh Schmidt, *The Religious History of America: The Heart of the American Story From Colonial Times to Today* (San Francisco, CA: HarperSanFrancisco, 2004), 424.

41 Bellah et al., *Habits of the Heart*, 228.

42 See Delbanco, *The Real American Dream*.

43 Ibid., 103.

44 Gaustad and Schmidt, 426.

45 Jonathan Haidt, *The Righteous Mind: Why Good People Are Divided by Politics and Religion* (New York: Vintage, 2013), esp. ch. 3.

46 Minsu Ha, David L. Haury, and Ross H. Nehm, "Feeling of Certainty: Uncovering a Missing Link Between Knowledge and Acceptance of Evolution," *Journal of Research in Science Teaching* 49 (2011): 95–121.

47 Robert Bellah, Richard Madsen, William Sullivan, Ann Swidler, and Steven Tipton, *Habits of the Heart* (Berkeley, CA: University of California Press, 1985), 221.

48 Wikipedia, "Sheilaism," https://en.wikipedia.org/wiki/Sheilaism, accessed 13 June 2019.

49 Mellisa M. Wilcox, "When Sheila's a Lesbian: Religious Individualism Among Lesbian, Gay, Bisexual, and Transgender Christians," *Sociology of Religion* 63, no. 4 (2002): 497–513.

50 Philip Clayton, "Religion and Views on Climate and Energy Issues," www.pewresearch.org/science/2015/10/22/religion-and-views-on-climate-and-energy-issues/, accessed 20 May 2022.

51 Sarah M. Pike, "Sarah Pike on Burning Man."

52 Albert R. Antosca, "Thinking Outside the Old Religious Box," 21 March 2018, *Slate*, https://slate.com/technology/2018/03/transhumanism-is-complicating-the-relationship-between-faith-and-science.html, accessed 20 May 2022.

53 This conversation was recorded privately via Zoom in spring 2022 and subsequently rechecked with Ecklund and edited for clarity.

54 Greg Cootsona, "Some Ways," esp. 568–70.

55 A good summary is found in Parson's *Being Spiritual but Not Religious: Past, Present, Future(s)* (London and New York: Routledge, 2018) and in his conversation with Fuller and Kirpal at Harvard Divinity School, "The Future of 'Spiritual But Not Religious,'" www.youtube.com/watch?v=0g2SSczJ_XI, accessed 14 May 2022.

56 Linda Mercadante, "Belief without Borders: Inside the Minds of the Spiritual But Not Religious," in *Being Spiritual But Not Religious*, ed. Parsons, 118–21.

57 Ecklund and Di, "Global Spirituality among Scientists," in *Being Spiritual But Not Religious*, ed. Parsons, 172.

58 Ibid., 170.

4 More than mindfulness
Buddhism and science

Buddhists represent less than 1% of the US population and about 7% of the world population.[1] Nevertheless, in how to relate religion to science, the Buddhist influence is outsized. According to Philip Clayton, a leading thinker in science and religion, Buddhism has become the "poster child for successfully integrating religion and science."[2] Alister McGrath, Oxford University Professor of Science and Religion, adds, "It is generally considered that Buddhism offers a particularly constructive relationship with the natural sciences."[3] And according to research by sociologists Elaine Howard Ecklund and Christopher Scheitle, "52 percent of Buddhists . . . are very interested in new scientific discoveries."[4]

In short, Buddhist thought seems well poised to flourish in an age of science and technology.

YouTube videos about the topic of Buddhism and science are too numerous to summarize, but I can highlight three key books: the Dalai Lama's *The Universe in a Single Atom: The Convergence of Science and Spirituality*,[5] which is noteworthy at least because it is penned by a Buddhist leader of worldwide stature; *Buddhism and Science: Breaking New Ground*, edited by B. Alan Wallace,[6] one of the most sustained and scholarly work to date; and more recently, Robert Wright's *Why Buddhism is True: The Science and Philosophy of Meditation and Enlightenment*, which makes a particularly fascinating connection between Buddhism and evolutionary psychology (and is quite bold about Wright's view of Buddhism).[7]

Still, probably the most best-known example, amalgamating modern physics (especially quantum mechanics) with "Eastern mysticism" (and, yes, the quotation marks are a hint of where this paragraph is headed) is Fritjof Capra's *The Tao of Physics*, a text first published almost half a century ago. Capra quite happily merges Buddhism and Daoist metaphysics on his tour through science. It's an enjoyable book, and Capra's presentation is clear and compelling, but the amalgamation that Capra presents rounds off some hard edges. It also strikes me as simple, far too simple.

DOI: 10.4324/9781003214236-4

It's worth citing Alfred North Whitehead again, "Seek simplicity and distrust it."[8] Whitehead's motto also makes our brief journey into Buddhism and science much more remarkable—and enlightening.

Introducing Buddhism: the lightning round Q & A

If you are a reader who needs a refresher on the basics of Buddhism that you learned years ago—or perhaps never at all—let's start with a lightning round question and answer on a religion founded more than 2,500 years ago in India.

What are the origins and history of Buddhism?

Traditionally, Siddhartha Gautama, a prince also known as Shakyamuni, or "Sage of the Shakya Clan," was probably born in 563 BCE in modern-day Nepal. Though royal and privileged, he found that he could not account for suffering and death. From this experience, he developed his famous Four Noble Truths (next). Thus, he became "the Buddha," a title—not a name—that means "the Awakened One." Siddhartha Gautama died at age 80, having consumed bad meat placed in his begging bowl. His final words were, "Impermanent are all formations. Observe this carefully, constantly."[9]

What is the problem and what is the solution that Buddhism presents?

We all suffer, but this reality can be overcome through following the Four Noble Truths.

What are the Four Noble Truths and the Eightfold Path?

These Truths are that all life is suffering, which is based on desiring that which cannot last nor satisfy, that suffering can be ended, if we follow the Eightfold Path—namely right speech, right action, right livelihood (ethical conduct), right effort, right livelihood, right mindfulness (mental discipline), right understanding, and right thought (wisdom). I love Boston University scholar of religion Stephen Prothero's summary of the Eightfold Path: "In short, be kind, be wise, be mindful."[10]

What is the question that Buddhism answers?

Prothero, as I've mentioned, argues that the key to understanding a religion is what question it seeks to answer.[11] What does Buddhism seek to answer about the human situation and life's purpose? To avoid *suffering* and gain enlightenment and release from cycle of rebirth, or at least attain a better rebirth by gaining merit.

I know about Catholics and Protestants; is there a similar distinction in Buddhism?

The earliest branch is Theravada, but the larger one, Mahayana—in fact called "the Greater Vehicle"—has more followers. And yet the most prominent in American minds—because of the fame of the Dalai Lama—is probably Tibetan Buddhism or Vajrayana, the smallest branch of the three. I could add Zen Buddhism, which derives from Mahayana and originated later in China and integrates Daoism and other forms of thought.

Now this is beginning to sound religious: Is there an afterlife in Buddhism?

Yes, there is reincarnation until we gain enlightenment and release. But curious—and in distinction from Hinduism—there is no surviving soul.

What then, is Buddhism soulless?

That's an affirmative. The Buddha said Yes to no soul, nor self. This is the complicated and confusing (at least for western thinkers) teaching of *anatman* in Sanskrit. I'll take another look at this later.

Does Buddhism have gods?

It depends—Theravada Buddhism is nontheistic, as is Buddhism generally, though Mahayana developed some elements of polytheism, and various Buddhas that serve as deities in function, if not even in fact.

Do you have to be exclusively Buddhist?

No—in this sense, it is quite different from monotheistic religions. One of the key locations for Buddhism, China, blends it with Confucianism and Daoism. These three religions are often combined in the United States as well.

What are key practices?

Certainly, meditation—but less common than those outside Buddhism might think—as well as mantras, devotion to deities (in some sects), and mandalas (particularly in Tibetan Buddhism).

How about central texts?

They are numerous, but neither "divinely inspired" nor "canonical" (to use Christian categories). Particularly relevant for this chapter are the Tripitaka (Pali Canon) and the Mahayana sutras like the Lotus Sutra.

How many Buddhists are there worldwide?

The estimates range, but over 500 million or about 7% of the world's population. Remembering the wisdom of Dr. Daniel Veidlinger—whom I'll introduce later—the number of Buddhists depends on what constitutes a Buddhist. The influence of Buddhist ideas on many Americans, in varying forms, is far beyond the 1% of our population that is Buddhist.

And how many American Buddhists are in the sciences?

According to Elaine Ecklund et al.'s 2015 RASIC study, Buddhists represent 2 % of scientists in this country.[12]

Daniel Veidlinger guides our journey

I've invited another scholar to accompany me on this journey—another whose knowledge will help me not to veer off the path of my Academic Hippocratic Oath. Dr. Daniel Veidlinger chairs the Comparative Religion and Humanities Department at Chico State University, where I teach and where he participated in a recent conference, "Science and Religions."[13] He's a bit of raconteur, and I can hear his Canadian-inflected voice down the halls of our department as he chats with colleagues on a variety of topics—of course, about Asian religion, but also his trips to India and Afghanistan, Russian politics during the Bolshevik Revolution, as well as alternative music. On that final topic, when Veidlinger required music for a new podcast he's creating, he created his own *original* compositions for the job. In fact, we put together a progressive rock trio for a jam session with Veidlinger on bass, me on drums, and a department colleague on guitar. (If this book comes out as a movie, maybe we'll play the soundtrack.)

Veidlinger specializes particularly in Buddhism and technology,[14] and his contributions weave in and through this chapter. Still, I haven't been able to persuade him that any great insights about Buddhism and science are *mine*, and any egregious mistakes are *his*. (Nor, I supposed, should I try to convince you.)

Caveats

My task in this chapter is to describe the relationship between Buddhism and science, highlighting the scientific and technological insights and discoveries that are particularly relevant to this religion. I learned in my earliest years to eat spinach first because then I'd really enjoy what's left on the plate. Similarly, before heading to enjoyable topics, I will deal initially with the challenges of the task in front of me by noting three caveats.

First, I need to return to the definitions of science. It's easy to lean on a western concept, reflecting the enduring contributions of the sixteenth and seventeenth-century European Scientific Revolution (and the seventeenth- and eighteenth-century Enlightenment). And though, even within the European–North American context, there is some variability, we can generally call this modern science.[15] Along those lines and in order to make this chapter manageable, I've kept a broad vision of Buddhism globally, while setting my focus on the United States. Still, since Buddhism is fundamentally an Asian religious tradition.[16]

Next, as I've mentioned, I am not assuming monotheistic or Abrahamic religion, nor its morality and broader metaphysics. It's not even self-evident that Buddhism constitutes a "religion," and so I'm cautious— but not unwilling—to apply "religion and science" in this chapter and indeed, throughout this book. Buddhism's defiance toward these definitions may be a rebellion against western colonialism. Wallace comments, "It is true that Buddhism fails to fit neatly into any of our categories of religion, philosophy, and science, for the simple reason that it did not develop in the West, where these concepts originated and evolved."[17]

Buddhism has one other act of resistance—namely, against the conflict narrative that has dominated discussions of religion and science in the United States. As Ecklund et al. have observed in *Science and Secularity* from their study of over 20,000 scientists worldwide, "*the conflict perspective on science and religion is an invention of the West.*"[18]

Another caveat is about descending from generalities into specificity. When I attempt to respond to the question of what "Buddhists think," Veidlinger wanted to be sure I got kept a key fact in mind:

> Buddhism is even less centralized than other religions, so it is hard to say what "Buddhists" think, both descriptively as there are just so many different groups that call themselves Buddhist, and even normatively as the canonical texts themselves are more diverse and multivocal than those of any religion.[19]

And so again, let's seek simplicity, but distrust it.

Finally, my presentation is vulnerable to the charge of presenting what Clayton calls "minimal Buddhism"—also called "Buddhist modernism," a weakness I can't entirely avoid. This is the flip side of the profound variations within Buddhism. Why not just make everything simple by finding the common core of tradition, where all the circles in the Venn Diagram overlap? Here's that particular caveat: *Be careful, the 'Buddhism' you're discussing might be "minimal Buddhism,"*[20] which—and now I quote Clayton—"emphasizes mindfulness and ethical living over traditional religious belief and practice."[21] It's contained in the slogan I've frequently heard that "Buddhism is primarily a science of the mind," or even the broadest and blandest form of "Buddhism brought us mindfulness." This represents a kind of lowest common denominator that contradicts very few ideas because it really makes so few commitments.

Buddhist modernism reduces Buddhism to *one* of its expressions, according to religious studies scholar David McMahan. It is also not "all Buddhism that happens to exist in the modern era, but, rather, forms of Buddhism that have emerged out of an engagement with the dominant cultural and intellectual forces of modernity."[22] Importantly, this is often presented as uniquely compatible with modern science, especially neuroscience, cognitive science, and psychology. It is often focused on mindfulness meditation and entails a minimalization of specific rituals and doctrine. Given the pressures of a disenchanted world—one suspect of religious discourse—it presents a sensible, this-worldly Buddhism.

Put another way, McMahan writes, "this articulation provides a distinctively modern way of resacralizing the world without resorting to the supernatural."[23] It similarly strikes University of British Columbia philosophy of mind professor Evan Thompson, who has spent significant time with Buddhist leaders including the Dalai Lama, to fall into "Buddhist exceptionalism," that is, "the belief that Buddhism is superior among the world religions in being inherent rational and empirical."[24] If I were so inclined, I could find another angle on the problem of minimalism in that, as Buddhist scholar Donald S. Lopez Jr. argues, the "image of scientific Buddhism is only about 150 years old."[25]

This Scylla of minimalism indeed, in a book of this length, is unavoidable. By naming it, though, I hope to steer clear of the Charybdis of saying nothing and missing the considerable contributions of Buddhism. In and through this chapter, let it not be forgotten that I'm seeking literacy in the conversation between this religious tradition and science.

Neuroscience, consciousness, and mindfulness

Why are science and Buddhism hot right now? The key reason is the relationship between Buddhist meditation—especially mindfulness—and its validation by neuroscience. Leaning on the ancient practice of *vipassana*, contemporary mindfulness meditation has some strong correlations with mental health and well-being.[26] Consider what University of Wisconsin psychologist Richard Davidson and his team have found (and now I quote Philip Clayton) "Those with training and practice in meditation showed greater activity in areas of the brain dedicated to paying attention and making decisions."[27]

Moreover, the tricky Buddhism concept of "no soul"—*anatman* or *anatta*—has striking resonance with contemporary neuroscience. Many neuroscientists find no enduring soul in their experimentation, but merely an ongoing presentation of a subjective "self." Here, I would agree with Veidlinger, who observes,

> I think the modern view has not yet found a soul, so certainly the idea that we are a conglomeration of various different forces all working together moment by moment to create a sense of the self is in accord with modern science.

Thompson agrees, "And from a neuroscience perspective, the brain and body is constantly in flux. There's nothing that corresponds to the sense that there's an unchanging self."[28]

There are two caveats. Mindfulness is certainly important for Buddhism. It's part of the Eightfold Path appearing as "right mindfulness." Still, I must report that, when I've been in academic meetings with Buddhists and the topic of mindfulness comes up, I often hear frustration or at least puzzlement. It's generally along the lines: "This isn't the fullness of Buddhist practice. There's a lot more to Buddhism than simply mindfulness." Or "do the people promoting mindfulness as an activity separate from Buddhism generally know what they're doing?" (This naturally is phrased in a more careful and academic way.)

In addition, I do need to add that something I've learned in conversations with leading Cognitive Science of Religion thinker Justin Barrett: it's not at all clear that the tools of neuroscience would ever find something non-material.[29] To paraphrase a saying attributed to Albert Einstein, "Not everything that's worth measuring can be measured." I'll leave it to Veidlinger to offer more sagacious insights and thus nuance,

> Some of the aggregates that make us up in the Buddhist view are non-material; for example, consciousness is a thing that is separable from the body in many understandings of Buddhism. And science would not agree with that, but in general certainly there is more accord than disagreement on *anatman*.

With that said, when most people I meet tell me about their reasons for concluding Buddhism is the most scientifically compatible religion, they most often highlight mindfulness. But as I've titled this chapter, Buddhism is about more than mindfulness.

Testing for truth

It would be hard to count how many times my ears have heard this sentence in conversations about science and religion (and I addressed this in Chapter 2 on Christianity): "Science tests until it finds truth, while religions rely on faith in ancient texts."

This common slogan has some obvious errors generally, but even more when considering Buddhism. Not all religious traditions emphasize faith—and even more blind fideism, which renders a blanket anti-religious cavil against "faith" a category error. Buddhism focuses on *awakening* or *enlightenment*, since indeed the word *Buddha* has as its root "awaken" or "enlighten." For this and other reasons, Buddhism and science seem to dance in a brilliant duet. It's why their connection will continue to draw interest.

But faith in what? Some conflicts between science and religion flare up around *sacred texts*, especially with western religions. Another gauntlet laid down by those who see an enduring "warfare"[30] between science and religion is this: there is a perverse and anti-rational element in religion since they look to their ancient texts. Religion texts always look back, but science continually looks forward. In this respect, Buddhism offers an openness to change its teachings based on new information. *Sutras* or *suttas* are purported to be the actual words of the Buddha himself, and with that in mind, this is from the Kalama Sutra (ca. 250 BCE),

> Do not go upon what has been acquired by repeated hearing; nor upon tradition; nor upon rumor; nor upon what is in a scripture; nor upon surmise; nor upon an axiom; nor upon specious reasoning; nor upon a bias towards a notion that has been pondered over; nor upon another's seeming ability; Rather, when you yourselves know that these things are good; these things are not blamable; undertaken and observed, these things lead to benefit and happiness, then and only then enter into and abide in them.[31]

And this corresponds well with the Dalai Lama who commented (a bit more recently than the sutra):

> Suppose that something is definitely proven through scientific investigation, that a certain hypothesis is verified, or a certain fact emerges as a result of scientific investigation. And suppose, furthermore, that that fact is incompatible with Buddhist theory. There is no doubt that we must accept the result of the scientific research.[32]

These statements are profound in its declaration of openness (and it parallels Pope John Paul II's statement about evolution). Similarly, Harvard University Professor of Comparative Religion and Indian Studies, Diana Eck concludes that "there is a common agenda and method in the fact that both mind science of the Buddhist tradition and the exploration of the medical researchers are based on the traditions of experimentation. [Buddhism is] an experimental practice."[33]

There are some limits to Buddhist openness to science, to which I'll return in a moment.

On nothingness and physics

Seinfeld became a TV hit for being a show "about nothing." But maybe Jerry Seinfeld and his colleagues were on to something. Buddhist discourse about "nothing" can be truly something worth listening to. Many commentators have expounded on Buddhist thought and science at the nexus of nothing, that is, emptiness.

In this case, to exegete words is to harvest intellectual fruit. One of the two Ur languages of Buddhism, Sanskrit, contributes the word *shunyata* which can be translated as "hollow, hollowness," "voidness," or "emptiness." It is nominal form, it is related to the adjective *shunya*, meaning "zero" (remember that[34]), "nothing," "empty," or "void." The root of both, *shvi*, means "hollow," and with the ending *ta*, means "-ness."

So far, so good. But I must admit feeling at least a modicum of trepidation. Prothero has stated that this teaching of emptiness presents innumerable difficulties, not only for his students but for Buddhism sages themselves like the third century CE Indian Buddhism philosopher Nagarjuna, "*Shunyata* misunderstood is like a snake grasped by the head."[35]

I am summarily warned and will therefore turn to science. Contemporary physics—especially quantum theory—has striking and counter-intuitive conclusions that connect with this teaching of emptiness, especially in Madhyamaka or the "middle way" of Mahayana Buddhism. Trained at the California Institute of Technology in physics, the Buddhist scholar William Ames has commented, "We recall that in quantum theory many of the properties of, for instance, an electron is not intrinsic to the electron itself. They depend not only on the electron but also on the type of experiment that is being performed."[36] Indeed, the famous two-slit experiment demonstrates that photons can behave as both a wave (as at a beach or in a bathtub) and particles (like bullets). Following Neils Bohr, one of the principal architects of quantum theory, who formulated the Concept of Complementarity: these are mutually exclusive descriptions, which are nonetheless both true. His coat of arms read "Opposites are complementary" (*Contraria sunt complementa*).[37] Ames continues with this observation, "In Madhyamaka, too, attributes are relational and not intrinsic. A dharma by itself has no nature, any more than an electron can in itself be said to be either a wave or a particle."[38]

Emptiness brings us to Heraclitus and the notion that we can't step into the same river twice. Whitehead, the mathematician of physics and later metaphysician at Harvard, sought to integrate Buddhism, Christianity, evolution, and relativity theory and developed what became known as process philosophy.[39] Whitehead, sounding very Madkyamakist, took this one step further: Because of the inexorable changes in the reality that is "us," *the same human* doesn't even step into the same river twice. Everything is constantly in process. Famously, Whitehead observed that Cleopatra's Needle, the obelisk in London, seems enduring, but given enough time, will certainly change and perish.[40]

This Buddhist focuses on nothing and emptiness has at least one more significant contribution. Here again I turn to Veidlinger, who remarked, "The zero was developed in India, in connection with philosophical speculation about emptiness, and it *is* the Indian number system that was adapted by the West that led to the notation used in the modern scientific world." One could even say (as I think he did) that the whole binary system of modern computer technology, with its 1s and 0s, ultimately depends on this insight.

An interlude: Buddhism and Big Bang

Despite Buddhism's science-friendly posture, the Dalai Lama, the Tibetan Buddhist leader, has noted problems with another key feature of Big Bang cosmology, which derives from Einstein's early-twentieth-century relativity theories, particularly general relativity. Though Einstein hated the conclusions so much that he fudged the equations with the "cosmological constant," mathematician Georges Lemaître and astronomer Edwin Hubble convinced him that indeed the universe was expanding. It has an initial point at about 13.7 billion years ago—the Big Bang—where time began (or $t = 0$).

Einstein had difficulties because of his philosophical commitment to the eternality of the universe in Spinoza's philosophy, and he is joined, for other reasons, by the Dalai Lama.

> From the Buddhist perspective, the idea that there is a single definite beginning is highly problematic. If there were such an absolute beginning, logically speaking, this leaves only two options. One is theism, which proposes that the universe is created by an intelligence

that is totally transcendent, and therefore outside the laws of cause and effect. The second option is that the universe came into being from no cause at all. Buddhism rejects both these options. If the universe is created by a prior intelligence, the questions of the onto-logical status of such an intelligence and what kind of reality it is remain.[41]

It's not entirely clear that Big Bang cosmology will last forever, or how alternative theories will fare, but the importance of the Dalai Lama's statement remains its assertion that Buddhism, at least in the Tibetan variety, is not infinitely open to scientific insight. How to apply the conclusions from the last section—"listen to science"—with this, some-thing akin to "faith" or at least "an enduring philosophical commit-ment" presents a conundrum, which I leave unanswered here. But I have another one.

On a related note, deeply embedded in Buddhist cosmology is the concept of karma. And when I passed my early ideas for this chapter to Veidlinger, he emphasized "don't forget the importance of karma" in Buddhism. So, I won't. I'll place it here.

Certainly, the Dalai Lama connects karma with the very nature of the cosmos, "Inherent in both the Kalachakra and Abhidharma cosmologies is the idea that the formation of a particular universe system is intimately connected with the karmic properties of sentient beings."[42] And only the "Buddha's omniscient mind"[43] can understand this—in the actions of sentient beings lies the nature of our cosmos. Karma therefore ultimately exists in a truly metaphysical—by which I mean more than physical—state. One can add that any scientific verification for karma or the bardo state after death in Tibetan Buddhism, which by nature exists outside of nature, is thus outside the realm of scientific investigation. Testing by sci-ence remains elusive and probably impossible. It softens the assertion that Buddhism is an entirely "scientific" religion because these are both vital Buddhist concepts.

Digital Buddhism

I offered separate definitions of science and technology, but they are deeply and often inextricably interconnected, a fact exemplified in the technological breakthroughs of genetics or of artificial intelligence (AI)—is that science *or* technology? It seems to be both. In this section, I again lean more on my interlocutor, Veidlinger, because the relationship between Buddhism and technology possesses a profound and surprising history, as well as present.

Buddhists have been content to use the latest technology to further their religious ideas. This got its start in Buddhist monasteries where monks printed the first book in 868 CE. It was the famous *Diamond Sutra*, printed in order to spread Buddhist teachings six centuries earlier than the printing press came to the west and Gutenberg printed his first Bible in 1455. Similarly, paper was developed in Buddhist monasteries.

Why did Buddhists develop paper to print their teachings? The religious impetus to develop these and other technologies represents a critical feature of their development. As Veidlinger commented,

> Even people who feel that religion has been detrimental to science have to remember that whether or not that's the case, many technological developments emerged through religious people who were trying to spread their religion, and along the way, develop these technologies.

This of course is carried forward today in "digital Buddhism"[44] (and paralleled the "new Gutenberg" of the internet, also employed by Christians through YouVersion and Biblegateway).

Evolution and the ethics of *ahimsa*

I am drawn again to the insights of sociologist John Evans—that the lion's share of conflicts between science and religion happens at the level of "morals, not knowledge" (to appropriate the title of his recent book[45]). This conflict obviously rears its head in certain monotheistic religious beliefs about God's creation and evolutionary biology. In this view, it's not simply that the Bible tells us we are uniquely created in God's image. Instead, it's about what that means for how we treat the rest of creation; we can exploit it.

Buddhists don't start with this particular commitment to inerrant sacred scripture or with a widespread rejection of evolution. In fact, about 81% of American Buddhists accept evolution.[46] Pew Research states quite simply and notes the implications,

> Many Buddhists see no inherent conflict between their religious teachings and evolutionary theory. Indeed, according to some Buddhist thinkers, certain aspects of Darwin's theory are consistent with some of the religion's core teachings, such as the notion that all life is impermanent.[47]

Moreover, if one begins with the connection of all sentient life, then it's not hard to find links with evolution. Buddhist scholar Inoue Enryo argues that Buddhism can embrace evolutionary thought because it holds to "no sharp distinction between humans and animals as Christians claim."[48]

In addition, since all sentient beings share a form of ethical equality, it is therefore no grand step to the Buddhist ethic of *ahimsa*, or nonviolence, to all sentient beings. *Ahimsa* anchors much of Buddhist ethics. It can, however, come into conflict with the practice of modern scientific research. Ecklund and her colleagues recorded a Taiwanese biologist commenting, "Buddhism is about not killing"[49] and that this comes into conflict with common scientific practice. What do scientists do when faced with tests on laboratory rats, for example? Noel Sheth, professor of Indian Philosophies and Religions, explains this divergence between Buddhism and modern science.

> For instance, many Buddhists are against organ transplants. They do not agree that the absence of brain activity indicates the death of a person because they connect life with the activity of the heart and lungs. As long as a body is warm, it is said to have life. They are also generally wary of genetic engineering, which appears to interfere with the karmic relationships between past generations and future generations.[50]

It can even be argued that modern science derives its practices from the notorious conclusion by Enlightenment philosophy Rene Descartes that human beings, because they are unique, can be "masters and possessors" of nature.[51] Buddhist ethics sets out a quite different path.

Final thoughts

I've written this book with the conviction that, unless religious traditions are able to integrate science and technology, those traditions will gradually fade. This isn't *per se* a full capitulation to the well-worn "secularization thesis" associated with sociologist Max Weber[52]—that science inevitably takes many of the traditional functions of religion—but it is a recognition that religions retain their vitality as they engage contemporary culture and that science is key cultural player. We have to see that religious insights make a difference—that what they say lands with our daily lives. Minimally, this rubric guides me in analyzing how any particular religion relates to contemporary science and vice versa.

How does Buddhism do? Is it truly Clayton's "poster child for successfully integrating religion and science"? Recognizing the stunning variety within Buddhism, I can't provide a summary statement for all Buddhists. But here are a few notes along the way. Surveys indicate that Buddhists tend not to integrate science with their religious life but generally describe religion and science as "two separate and unrelated spheres," according to the Pew Research Center.[53] Buddhism is generally nontheistic, or minimally it has no teaching of a God as Creator, which is a theological affirmation that has proven problematic for elements of modern scientific cosmology. Still, as we saw with the Big Bang, there are limits to its engagement. Moreover, because it is rooted in East Asian culture, Buddhism is less historically emerged in a conflict with western science. Most striking is the Buddha's openness to experimentation (though not absolute), the connection between Buddhist views of self in light of contemporary neuroscience, and the confirmation via scientific studies that meditation is beneficial for physical and mental health.

All in all, Buddhism may not represent *the* poster child. Still, I'll affirm that for a tradition that's been around 2,500 years, it's doing remarkably well at sounding notes that ring harmoniously with contemporary science. Buddhism will continue to make significant contributions to the ways that we negotiate the relationship between science and religion. From what I see, its influence indeed is on the rise.

Suggestions for further reading

For an incisive overview of Buddhism and science, the collection of essays edited by Alan B. Wallace is an excellent place to start, *Buddhism and Science: Breaking New Ground* (New York: Columbia University Press, 2003) as is Donald J. Lopez Jr., *Buddhism and Science: A Guide for the Perplexed* (Chicago, IL: University of Chicago Press, 2008). For a bit more fun, see Lopez, *The Scientific Buddha: His Short and Happy Life* (New Haven, CT and London: Yale University Press, 2012). To grasp the essence of Buddhism modernism, I recommend Evan Thompson's *Why I Am Not a Buddhist* (New Haven, CT and London: Yale University Press, 2020) as well as David McMahan, *The Making of Buddhist Modernism* (Oxford: Oxford University Press, 2016).

For more of an insider look at Buddhism and science, both Dalai Lama, *The Universe in a Single Atom: The Convergence of Science and Spirituality* (New York: Harmony, 2006), and Robert Wright, *Why Buddhism Is True: The Science and Philosophy of Meditation and Enlightenment* (New York: Simon & Schuster, 2018), will do the trick. And finally, to grasp the Buddhism and contemporary technology, the collected edited by Daniel Veidlinger is excellent, *Digital Humanities and Buddhism* (Berlin: de Gruyter, 2019).

Notes

1 *World Population Review,* "Buddhist Countries 2022," https://worldpopulationre-view.com/country-rankings/buddhist-countries, accessed 15 June 2022.

2 Philip Clayton, *Religion and Science: The Basics,* 2nd ed. (New York: Routledge, 2019), 53.

3 McGrath, *Science and Religion: A New Introduction,* 2nd ed. (Oxford: Wiley-Black-well, 2010), 140.

4 Elaine Howard Ecklund and Christopher Scheitle, *Religion vs. Science: What Religious People Really Think* (Oxford: Oxford University Press, 2018), 19.

5 Dalai Lama, *The Universe in a Single Atom: The Convergence of Science and Spirituality* (New York: Morgan Road Books, 2005).

6 Alan B. Wallace, ed., *Buddhism and Science: Breaking New Ground* (New York: Columbia University Press, 2003).

7 Robert Wright, *Why Buddhism Is True: The Science and Philosophy of Meditation and Enlightenment* (New York: Simon & Schuster, 2018).

8 A. N. Whitehead, *The Concept of Nature* (Cambridge: Cambridge University Press, 1930), 46.

9 Novak, *The World's Wisdom,* 62.

10 Prothero, *God Is Not One: The Eight Rival Religions That Run the World* (New York: HarperOne, 2010), 183.

11 Ibid., chapter 1.

12 *Secularity and Science,* 30.

13 Veidlinger, "Buddhist Attitudes Towards Science and Technology," https://media.csuchico.edu/media/Buddhist+Attitudes+Towards+Science+and+Techn ology/0_r023i0xy, accessed 15 June 2022.

14 E.g., Veidlinger, *Digital Humanities and Buddhism* (Berlin: de Gruyter, 2019); *Buddhism, the Internet, and Digital Media: The Pixel in the Lotus,* Routledge Studies in Religion and Digital Culture (New York: Routledge, 2014).

15 See Greg Cootsona, *Negotiating Science and Religion* (New York: Routledge, 2020), chapter 2; Tomoko Yoshida and Stephen P. Weldon, "Asian Traditions," in *Science and Religion: A Historical Introduction,* 2nd ed., ed. Gary B. Ferngren (Baltimore, MD: Johns Hopkins, 2017), 315.

16 Yoshida and Weldon, "Asian Traditions," 213.

17 Wallace, "Introduction: Buddhism and Science—Breaking Down Barriers," in *Buddhism and Science,* 6.

18 Elaine Howard Ecklund et al., *Science and Secularity: What Scientists Around the World Really Think About Religion* (Oxford: Oxford University Press, 2019), 9, italics in the original.

19 These citations, unless otherwise noted, are taken from our email interchanges and used by permission.

20 See also, David McMahan, *The Making of Buddhist Modernism* (Oxford: Oxford University Press, 2016).

21 Philip Clayton, *Science and Religion: The Basics,* 53–5.

22 McMahan, 6.

23 Ibid., 218.

24 Evan Thompson, *Why I Am Not a* Buddhist (New Haven, CT: Yale University Press, 2020), 25.

25 "Asian Traditions" noting *The Scientific Buddha: His Short and Happy Life,* in Ferngren, 317.

26 Amishi P. Jha, "Being in the Now," March/April 2013, www.scientificamerican. com/index.cfm/_api/render/file/?method=inline&fileID=B5A4B49C-45A3-4CA0-BE616040A83EAA2C, accessed 15 June 2022.

27 Clayton, 56.

28 Olivia Goldhill, "Neuroscience Backs Up the Buddhist Belief That 'The Self' Isn't Constant, But Ever-Changing," 2015 *Quartz*, https://qz.com/506229/neuroscience-backs-up-the-buddhist-belief-that-the-self-isnt-constant-but-ever-changing.

29 Private conversation.

30 Cf. Andrew Dickson White and Timothy Draper's texts. But also, cf. Jeff Hardin et al., eds., *The Warfare Between Science and Religion: The Idea That Wouldn't Die* (Baltimore, MD: Johns Hopkins, 2018).

31 Kalama Sutra, cited in Jake H. Davis and Owen Flanaga, *A Mirror Is for Reflection: Understanding Buddhist Ethics* (Oxford: Oxford University Press, 2017), 106–7.

32 In Wallace, *Buddhism and Science*, 77.

33 Diana Eck in Dalai Lama, Herbert Benson, Robert Thurman, Howard Gardner, Daniel Goleman, *MindScience: An East-West Dialogue* (Boston, MA: Wisdom, 1999), 106.

34 Monier-Williams, Sir Monier 2nd ed., *A Sanskrit-English Dictionary* (1899), reprinted (Delhi: Motilal Banarsidass, 1986), 1085.

35 Prothero, *God Is One*, 193, quoting Nagarjuna in Nancy McCagney, *Nagarjuna and the Philosophy of Openness* (Lanham, MD: Rowan & Littlefield, 1997), 34.

36 Ames, in Wallace, 301.

37 Capra, 160, who ties this in with Chinese philosophy and the ying-yang, which is intriguing.

38 Ibid.

39 His key—but very difficult—text is *Process and Reality*. See also Ryusei Takeda, "Whitehead Reconsidered from a Buddhist Perspective," in *Global Perspectives on Science and Spirituality*, ed. Pranab Das (West Conshohocken, PA: Templeton Press, 2009), 93.

40 Whitehead, *The Concept of Nature* (Cambridge: Cambridge University Press, 1930), 165–7.

41 Dalai Lama, 82.

42 Ibid., 90.

43 Ibid., 91.

44 See Veidlinger, ed., *Digital Humanities and Buddhism*.

45 Evans, *Morals, Not Knowledge: Recasting the Contemporary U.S. Conflict Between Religion and Science* (Berkeley, CA: University of California Press, 2018).

46 *Pew Research Center*, "Religious Differences on the Question of Evolution: Buddhism," updated 3 February 2014, www.pewforum.org/2009/02/04/religious-differences-on-the-question-of-evolution, accessed 15 June 2022.

47 *Pew Research Center*, "Religious Groups' Views on Evolution," www.pewforum. org/2009/02/04/religious-groups-views-on-evolution, accessed 15 June 2022.

48 "Asian Traditions," 323.

49 Ecklund et al., *Science and Secularity*, 190.

50 Sheth, Buddhism and Science, paper presented at 2004 Metanexus conference, www.metanexus.net/archive/conference2004/pdf/sheth.pdf, accessed 15 June 2022.

51 Rene Descartes, *Discourse on Method*, Part IV, www.bartleby.com/34/1/6.html, accessed 3 June 2022.

52 See Ecklund et al., *Science and Secularity*, 2; Max Weber, *The Protestant Ethic and the Spirit of Capitalism*, 3rd ed., trans. Stephen Kalberg (New York: Roxbury Publishing Co., 2002), esp. lxxx.

53 *Pew Research Center*, "On the Intersection of Science and Religion," www. pewforum.org/essay/on-the-intersection-of-science-and-religion, accessed 15 June 2022.

5 The way of interconnection

Science and nature religions

I've beta-tested a good deal of the material in this book with my college students at Chico State. And when I raise the topic of nature religions, my students seem to be listening a bit more intently. They sit up in their chairs. They want to know more. For them and many others, nature religions represent a viable, attractive alternative to Christianity. Nature religions emphasize an interconnection of human beings with the natural world and lean toward ecology, and specifically environmentalism, as the central form of science.

But it's not just in Chico. Colorado-based writer Molly Hanson, who writes on religion, ritual, and psychology, paints a provocative picture, and she employs the often-misunderstood term, "witch" (instead of more neutral term "wiccan") to catch our attention:

> The witch is impossible to ignore. Pop into an Urban Outfitters and you're sure to find an array of tarot card packs, a beginner's guide to crystals, and a spell book or two . . . . On Instagram, a popular #witchesofinstagram hashtag is now widely used, and the account @thehoodwitch has a following on the platform of over 434,000 followers.[1]

With that said, I do have one important warning before you begin: This particular chapter has the widest grouping of religions (if we can even use the term "religion" effectively for them). Nature religions include Wicca, Native American traditions, contemporary Paganism, nature spirituality, and New Age. It's exceedingly difficult to generalize about Paganism, let alone hundreds of American Indian tribes. To add further complexity, some who might be categorized as participating in nature religions might also consider themselves "Spiritual but Not Religious" (SBNR), which is another chapter. At the same time, many of the things I'll write here I could also ascribe to Hinduism. Indeed, overlap and interconnection are integral to American religion and spirituality.

DOI: 10.4324/9781003214236-5

In fact, every chapter in this book—for example, when I summarize Islam and its 1.8 billion followers—falls prey to generalization. But I will forge ahead, seeking to stay true to my Academic Hippocratic Oath ("cause no harm"). My intention is to not distort any of the particular traditions I'm including here. Even more, I hope to provide accurate and helpful insights into how nature religions interact with science because they bring unique insights and contributions. Are you ready?

Introducing nature religions: the lightning round Q & A

Note that this Q & A is a bit longer than some other chapters because I assume readers know less about these religious traditions.

What do I mean by "nature religions"?

These religions or traditions of spirituality connect with, and find sacredness in, the natural world. Thus, the divine is immanent (not transcendent). Sarah Pike (whom you'll meet later) has commented, "Nature religions are generally focused on the idea that gods and other supernatural powers can be found through the direct experience of natural events and natural objects." As scholar of religion Bron Taylor comments, "Nature religion is most commonly used as an umbrella term to mean religious perception and practices that are characterized by a reverence for nature and that consider its destruction a desecrating act."[2] Nature religions generally resist the view of a transcendent deity over and even against the natural world "because it leads to environmental degradation."[3] This might be the place to add (because it doesn't fit elsewhere) that this is a common conception of immanence—that it stands in utter contrast to transcendence. It's not entirely accurate: Islam emphasizes, perhaps more than any religion, God's transcendence, and yet the Quran speaks of God being "closer than [our] jugular vein" (Quran 50:16), which sounds surprisingly like an immanent Deity.

What is the problem and solution that nature religions present?

We have become disconnected from the natural world, and the solution is to reconnect with its sacredness. Something in fact is wrong until we restore our harmony with nature.

What about contemporary Paganism?

This is "a modern religious movement which seeks to incorporate beliefs or ritual practices from traditions outside the main world religions, especially those of pre-Christian."[4] I am including in this category contemporary Paganism traditions such as Wicca, Asatru, Heathens, and neo-Druidism. Need I add that this is quite different from a vernacular use of "pagan"? "An unconverted member of a people or nation who does not practice Christianity, Judaism, or one who has little or no religion and who delights in sensual pleasures and material goods: an irreligious or hedonistic person."[5] I've learned to make this clarification in my college classes because my students look confused when I mention Paganism.

Do these religions have a god or gods?

Nature traditions are quite varied: God or the Sacred can be monotheistic, duotheistic, pantheistic, animistic, polytheistic, or henotheistic (meaning worship of one God within a polytheistic context), and they are often a combination of these.

How many practitioners are there of nature religions?

Because these religions don't generally have the same structural characteristics as Christianity, for example, finding the number of members in nature religions is challenging. Pew estimates that there are 1.2 million contemporary Pagans in the United States.[6] In addition, "5.2 million American Indians and Alaska Natives registered in the U.S. Census."[7] (More broadly, Indigenous peoples number over 500 million throughout the globe.[8]) With that said, this might be the place to underline that many Native Americans practice Christianity and sometimes combine elements of traditional Native religion with it.[9]

Who are the founders of these religions?

Similar to Hinduism, these religions lack a key founder, like Muhammad for Islam or Siddhartha Gautama for Buddhism, though they may have key leaders who emerge over time, like Vine Deloria for Native Americans or Starhawk as a leading feminist Pagan. As important as people are events like Burning Man in Black Rock Desert, Nevada, or places like the Esalen Institute in California.

Is there any one thing that holds these various religions together?

One central idea is that all living beings—and sometimes inanimate things—are interconnected. To repeat, or as Hanson summarizes, "neo-pagans also follow a cosmology that understands the universe as an interconnected whole. All beings are linked with all the cosmos as part of a unified living organism."[10] Among other things, this also implies that life and death are interconnected realities. This is a key concept addressed in the following.

Learning from Sarah Pike on nature religions

As in other chapters, I've integrated insights from another scholar to accompany—one whose knowledge will help me not to veer off the path. Dr. Sarah Pike is a nationally recognized authority on nature religions. Thankfully she also works down the hall in the Comparative Religion and Humanities Department at California State University, Chico. And in this chapter, I'll also draw in another brilliant scholar from my department and specialist in this area, Sarah Gagnebin.

Dr. Pike has served as President of the International Society for the Study of Religion, Nature, and Culture, and not only she does her work at academic conferences and in conversation with other scholars but she also engages in fieldwork, combining ethnographic and historical methods, for example, at the well-known Burning Man Festival or in understanding contemporary environmental activism. At the 2017 Chico State Science and Religions conference, she presented "Science and Nature Religions," from which I draw some of her remarks.[11]

No specific words

Among these religions—and frankly, as we've discovered in other chapters—the two key words, "religion" and "science," are problematic, and yet, this fact offers insight. Specifically, there is often no specific word for "religion."[12] For example, according to Severin Fowles, Columbia University archeologist, the Southeast Pueblo word sometimes translated as "religion" is better rendered as "doing."[13] Religion is not separated from the rest of life. As Biologist and Tewa tribal member Gregory Cajete writes,

> The essence of native spirituality is not religion in the Western sense of the word, but rather a set of core beliefs in the sanctity of personal and community relationships in the natural world, which are creatively acted upon and expressed at both the personal and communal levels.[14]

Because there is a fluidity in connecting with, or sometimes critiquing, modern science, practitioners of nature religions a variety of terms, there are often no specific words that match modern science or even science more generally. Substitutes find their way into this discourse. Bucknell professor of ecology and religion John Grim employs the term *lifeways* as a descriptor, in contrast with "western science," or what I've been calling modern science in this book. (I will also highlight a related term, Traditional Knowledge, or TK, later.)

Put another way, as Pike has commented, these religions (and their worldviews and traditions) can be grouped together in that they "make nature their symbolic center."[15] Similarly, Grim writes:

> Lifeway is an interrogative concept that *raises questions* about the ways in which diverse indigenous communities celebrate, work towards, and reflect on their wholeness as a people. *Indigenous knowledge* is a key component in this reflection. In their diverse ways of knowing the world, indigenous peoples draw out their identity and meaning-in-the-world in both the presence of *ecosystems* and the authority of cosmology (italics mine).[16]

I italicized three key points so that I could highlight their importance: (1) Lifeways necessarily pose questions to the way we understand the world through what is commonly understood as science. (2) The imbedded knowledge of a people are key sources of insight, not only laboratory experimentation or findings from a research university. (3) The entire biological community of organisms interacting in their physical environment and this interconnected system—that is, the ecosystem—is involved.

According to Cajete, *Native science* can be viewed as

> a metaphor for a wide range of tribal processes of perceiving, thinking, acting, and "coming to know" that have evolved through human experience with the natural world. Native science is born of a lived and storied participation with the natural landscape. In its core experience, Native science is based on the perception gained from using the entire body of our senses in direct participation with the natural world.[17]

Science understood in this mode makes it akin to ecology, at least in the sense of environmentalism or sustainability. In addition, it is connected to spirituality. Cajete summarizes by saying that "Native science integrates a spiritual experience."[18]

Cajete lists 28 "methodological elements and tools of Native science,"[19] five of which are particularly relevant here. *Unity*: "Native science stresses order and harmony but also acknowledges diversity and chaos as creators of reality." *Spirit*: "Native science incorporates spiritual process: no division exists between science and spirituality." *Cosmology*: "[T]he universe was created along with humankind's emergence into the world." *Life energy* "acknowledged throughout the expressions of knowledge, understanding, and application." Finally, *Dreams and Visions* "are a natural means for accessing knowledge and establishing relationship to the world."

Cajete emphasizes that Native science is *relational*,[20] and that relationship is horizontal, not vertical. In other words, we are not *above* nature, but part of its interconnected reality. Scientists thus should not be distanced and separated from nature the subject, as has been the tradition in Europe and the United States since the Enlightenment, but deeply imbedded in the subject. An easy juxtaposition is seventeenth-century French philosopher Rene Descartes, a philosopher intimately linked with the rise of modern science and the Scientific Revolution in Europe. Descartes framed a famous and notorious phrase (which I just quoted in the previous chapter) that we are "masters and possessors" of nature.[21] In contrast, nature religions present human beings as not distinct from the natural world, thus standing over it and manipulating it at will. We find our way of knowing through the deep interconnection with the natural world, and this makes Native science "the most ancient sustainability science" according to Cajete[22] (a theme to which I will return).

Ethics as a starter

For the moniker of this chapter, I used "the way of interconnection," and that is an appropriate framing for the ethics of nature religions, which set humankind within the interconnected framework of nature as equal partners with other animals and other living beings. Thus, human beings should not practice science from outside or from above, but from *within*, with an emphasis on recognizing and reinforcing this interconnection.

It's particularly challenging to identify a separate ethical strand in this chapter because ethics are also part of this interconnection. Specifically, climate change and environmental care stand at the center of nature religions. Margot Adler, herself a contemporary Pagan, has written an important work on her tradition, *Drawing Down the Moon*, which refers to Wiccan ritual in which a High Priestess enters into a trance and asks that the Goddess, symbolized by the Moon, to enter her body and use her as a means to communicate. It's easy to see a connection and intermingling of the natural world—even in space—with our Earth. Accordingly, Adler finds a deep pagan connection with science that cares for the Earth, citing Leo Martello's definition: "Pagans are close to the earth, have a love for her, and are certainly concerned when she is polluted."[23] Science and technology should be used well, but not result in "desensitization" or in worship of science—"scientolatry"—or *scientism*, the viewpoint that science has the power and therefore obligation to describe all there is to know about the world.[24]

In addition, climate change and sustainability—in response to one by-product of the technology of modern science, namely, global degradation—have significant impact on Indigenous peoples and practitioners of nature religions. One national report noted, "Climate change threatens indigenous peoples' livelihoods and economies. Its impacts are projected to be especially severe for many of the almost 600 federally recognized tribes in the United States that depend on traditional places, foods, and lifestyles."[25] Indigenous knowledge was frankly better at caring for the Earth, and many today who look beyond modern science in responding to climate change.

I'll offer one concrete example in light of climate change as a representative document, "Guidelines for Considering Traditional Knowledges in Climate Change Initiatives."[26] The guidelines focus on two principles: "Cause No Harm" (indeed a form of the Hippocratic Oath) and "Free, Prior and Informed Consent" (be sure we know that we are part of the effects of some technological or scientific practice). And thus there is a restraint on the use of technology. "Technology should be appropriate and reflected a balanced relationship with the natural world."[27]

This obviously has direct connections with climate change, a topic that seamlessly fits with Indigenous science. My own home state of California, and particularly the northern part of the state where I live, has been hit repeatedly by wildfires, and we are looking to Native American traditions for how to practice manage burns and thereby mitigate the risk of these fires.

The method of story

The method of Native science, and many nature religions, relies on stories to communicate truth. This emphasis stands in contrast to much of Western thought with its emphasis on rational description and mathematical formulas. Instead, Native science places stories—and related terms like *metaphor*[28]—as fundamental. Cajete writes, "Native science is a story, an explanation of the ways of nature and sources of life, embedded in the guiding stories of a people and the language and way of life that convey their stories."[29] These are not static, but dynamic and even evolutionary. "In brief, Native people stories relate the evolution of the people through time, space, and place."[30] This will sometimes set the framework of Native science in contrast, or even contradiction, to the narratives of modern science and its methods.

Creation myths form a key component of these stories. Here—it is critical to note—I am using *myth* in the sense that religious scholars employ it—as "meaningful stories," and not as "fiction" or even "lies." Creation myths in Native and Indigenous cultures may in fact contradict one another from the perspective of philosophical analysis and formal logic. They are retold in ways that contain important truths for the tribes, but they also may or may have objective reference. In other words, these creation myths are not treated as a biblical literalist reads Genesis 1 on the creation of the world in 6 days, or a traditional Muslim interpreting of Quran's 15th surah about God's direct creation of Adam. Of course, I'm avoiding any hard-and-fast rules, but these stories as a whole offer narratives of origin.

Because these myths are unfamiliar to many, I'd like to cite or to summarize a few in some detail. For help, I emailed another colleague in comparative religion at Chico State, Sarah Gagnebin, and I asked her for key stories of origin for Paganism. Naturally, some modern Pagans turn to the standard scientific story of an evolving 13.7-billion-year-old universe, and some do not have any creation stories. (We return to the theme of the immense variety within Paganism.) Nonetheless, Gagnebin summarized,

> Since pagans tend to coalesce around certain historical traditions, each group might look to a different creation myth as their own. For example, modern Druids (Celtic pagans) look to the ancient Celtic myths involving the Tuatha De Danann a group of gods/primordial beings including, notably, a god called An Dagda. A leader of sorts in the battle that would decide who the creators of the Irish people would be. Heathens look to a creation story about Niflheim (Ice realm) and Muspelheim (fire realm), two realms that came out of a vast emptiness. The fire melted the ice and the drips created Ymir, the first giant. He grew other giants, there was a battle. All realms are connected by Yggrasil, the tree of life (their Axis Mundi).

Gagnebin told me that this holds for Roman pagan Reconstructionists, and many others. And then she added,

> The only over-arching pagan creation story that many pagan folks share is in the realm of Goddess worship or Dianic Wicca. This story begins with the great Goddess, the earth. She created all living things including people. The story goes that the original humans worshipped her and made millions of goddess figurines in her honor. This continued until the Indo-European invasions which brought a

dualistic religion with a male head-god, thus shattering the primordial Goddess worship. Goddess worship thus goes underground, but continues, and re-emerges in late 1800s. But certainly not all pagans subscribe to this creation myth.[31]

None of these then is canonical scripture. They are, nonetheless, evocative in narrating the world and our place in it.

Let's also consider just one of the many Native American creation myths, the Salinan Indian Creation Story, from an area that today is California.[32] I cite it, not because it's universal, but to exemplify a shared inclination to recognize spiritual power in the natural world.

When the world was finished, there were as yet no people, but the Bald Eagle was the chief of the animals. He saw the world was incomplete and decided to make some human beings. So he took some clay and modeled the figure of a man and laid him on the ground. At first he was very small but grew rapidly until he reached normal size. But as yet he had no life; he was still asleep. Then the Bald Eagle stood and admired his work. "It is impossible," said he, "that he should be left alone; he must have a mate." So he pulled out a feather and laid it beside the sleeping man. Then he left them and went off a short distance, for he knew that a woman was being formed from the feather. But the man was still asleep and did not know what was happening. When the Bald Eagle decided that the woman was about completed, he returned, awoke the man by flapping his wings over him and flew away.

The man opened his eyes and stared at the woman. "What does this mean?" he asked. "I thought I was alone!" Then the Bald Eagle returned and said with a smile, "I see you have a mate! Have you had intercourse with her?" "No," replied the man, for he and the woman knew nothing about each other. Then the Bald Eagle called to Coyote who happened to be going by and said to him, "Do you see that woman?" Try her first!" Coyote was quite willing and complied, but immediately afterwards lay down and died. The Bald Eagle went away and left Coyote dead, but presently returned and revived him. "How did it work?" said the Bald Eagle. "Pretty well, but it nearly kills a man!" replied Coyote. "Will you try it again?" said the Bald Eagle. Coyote agreed, and tried again, and this time survived. Then the Bald Eagle turned to the man and said, "She is all right now; you and she are to live together."[33]

Readers may note that this story shares some characteristics with the creation story in Genesis 1, for example, the original pair of a man and a woman. And this takes me to a bit of detour, but a relevant one: many Americans' default creation story is still the narrative from the first pages of the Bible. It strikes me that, when John Glenn landed on the Moon in 1969, he read the Genesis 1 story. Even with a diminishing Christian percentage of Americans, the words, "In the beginning, God created the heavens and earth" are familiar. They sound vernacular.

Indigenous stories are also strikingly different. Even when there are similar features, the interpretation heads in an alternative direction. In many Native American creation stories, human beings appear last in the story—which is similar to the Jewish narrative in Genesis where God creates Adam and Eve on the sixth day—but this does not lead to the *dominion* of human beings. Instead, it points to the necessity of our learning from other animals. Bestselling author, biologist, and member of the Citizen Potawatomi Nation Robin Wall Kimmerer writes that—as opposed to the foundational creation story in western monotheism,

> In Native ways of knowing, human people are often referred to as "the young brothers of Creation." We say that humans have the least experience with how to live and thus the most to learn—we must look to our teachers among the other species for guidance.[34]

And we continue to learn, for example, in Native American spirituality; we search a spirit animal as a practice that guides human life toward wisdom.

Kimmerer comments on another story from her elders that describes the Skyworld, Skywoman, and the importance of planting sweetgrass *wiingaaashk*, "the first to grow on the earth":

> Same species, same earth, different stories. Like Creation stories everywhere, cosmologies are a source of identify and orientation to the world. They tell us who we are. We are inevitably shaped by them no matter how distant they may be from our consciousness. One story leads to the generous embrace of the living world, the other to banishment. One woman is our ancestral gardener, a cocreator of the good green world that would be the home of her descendants. The other was an exile, just passing through an alien world on a rough road to her real home of heaven.[35]

Notably, Kimmerer's prose rings with overtones of superiority as she describes this approach to nature, a characteristic I highlight because it seems to be an indelible human trait even though Indigenous ways of knowing accept a wide variety of stories, where one is not ultimately canonical and therefore implicitly superior to others. Nevertheless, my larger point is that human beings are set within an interconnection with the wider world. There is also a notable lack of *speciesism*—the belief that human beings are unique and thus above all other animals. We return here to the theme of an interconnected and horizontal relationship with the rest of nature.

The spiritualization of science

Following the work of physicists like David Bohm and David Peat, nature religions—and particularly some Native American traditions[36]—draw on quantum physics. Cajete has written, "With the developing prominence of the theories of quantum mechanics and nonlocality, theoretical physicists like Peat have sensed that the universe has a nonmaterial, deep spiritual dimension, even and elegant guiding intelligence that has already been recognized within Native science."[37] The deep interconnection of reality described by some quantum physicists like Bohm and Peat provides a link with metaphysics of nature religions. For what it's worth, Bohm expressed an indebtedness to Eastern thought, especially the thought of the leading theosophical thinker Jiddu Krishnamurti, and to a lesser degree the Dalai Lama.[38] The directionality of this linking did not head directly from physics to an interconnected view of world—it was reciprocal.

To be clear, the prominent Copenhagen interpretation from the Danish scientist Niels Bohr, architect of the foundations of quantum theory, heads in a much less integrated and interconnected direction. He largely emphasized the problem of measurement and description of the quantum world: "Physics is not about how the world is, it is about what we can say about the world."[39] In addition, "unlike Bohm's theory, in the standard formulation, particles do not have definite positions and velocities, and there is no quantum potential."[40] Moreover, to make grand metaphysical conclusions did not strike Bohr as justified.

More broadly, there is the question of "quantum woo"[41] or the justification of irrational beliefs by vague reference to concepts in quantum physics such as quantum entanglement ("when two particles link together in a certain way no matter how far apart they are in space"[42]) and the related term nonlocality ("where there is no such thing as place or distance"[43]). Strongly leaning on entanglement and interconnection as a metaphysical principle builds off one interpretation of quantum physics, but certainly not all. It is not clear that quantum physics leads directly, or even unambiguously, to this particular metaphysics.

However nature religions do or do not connect with quantum physics, Pike has also raised the topic of a "spiritualization of science." Does science as practice and as a contributor to our understanding of the universe lead to a particular spirituality? As one example, Pike pointed to the Gaia hypothesis, which microbiologist Lynn Margulis and chemist James Lovelock first formulated in the 1970s, "that living organisms interact with their inorganic surroundings on Earth to form a synergistic and self-regulating, complex system that helps to maintain and perpetuate the conditions for life on the planet."[44] Despite subsequent clarifications to the contrary by Margulis, contemporary Pagans have often connected this hypothesis with their worship of Earth as a goddess.[45]

Questions that fascinate me

There are some remaining questions in bringing together these various nature religions with modern science and technology. How will newcomers to these religions relate to the embedded traditional knowledge of those who have practiced these traditions for millennia? How, for example, can an emerging generation, fed on shifting insights provided by the internet and seeking updated knowledge, relate to the "tradition of the elders" in Native American spirituality? Science tends to present itself as a continually progressive movement that replaces older ideas with new, more advanced ones, and this challenges really any religion.

How do nature religions connect with evolution, a mainstay of modern science? Some see a connection with the Native American myths. Cajete writes, "The idea of evolving, or changing through generations, is part of Indigenous thinking." And yet he adds, "But 'evolution' in Native thinking should not be understood in the Western way. Native people created their stories and explanations of how things came to be," and thus they are from "a particular viewpoint," not some universal scientific approach.[46] In another sense, evolution, thus interpreted, dethrones *Homo sapiens* as the crown of creation and thus allows for a deeper environmental ethic, a key component of nature religions.

Modern science is not neutral. The Scientific Revolution is directly related to colonizing non-European peoples. Developing weapons of war funded the advance of science and technology. Particularly, we cannot forget the profoundly disturbing historical encounter of Native Americans with modern technology. The development of western science in Europe, and thus the American colonies, produced extraordinary technological advances and weaponry, which is one means by which that the Native Americans were killed and colonized by European settlers.

Finally, there exists an ambiguity of some nature religions with modern science, especially as science is commonly practiced. Can we say that nature religions are anti-science? Pike remarked, "Even though in some ways they are anti-science in terms of the destructive effect of science on the earth, [nature religions] are still drawing on a lot of scientific research." We see this in the work of Kimmerer and Cajete, who trained in both western and Native science. Similarly, Hanson writes, "Neo-paganism might well be a reaction against what Max Weber referred to as the 'disenchantment of the world' whereby modern life and scientific advancement have drained a sense of the sacred from our lives."[47] This takes us back to resisting scientism and a subsequent recasting of western scientific practice.

Final thoughts

In terms of lived religion, what might this look like today? How might nature religions be practiced? Around the time I was trying to draw this chapter to a close, I found myself near the Washington, DC Mall, having just finished a formal convening and conversation about diversifying the dialogue of science and religion. This event was a striking reminder of the variety of religions and their approaches to science. How to pluralize the dialogue of science was on my mind as I walked. Outside the Museum of the American Indian, I passed by six people celebrating a Native American ceremony. I decided not to interrupt nor really to lurk uncomfortably around, but still to take in what I could. They were chanting and offering prayers, perhaps to reclaim a sacred location, one right outside a museum meant to honor their traditions. In the midst of our National Capital, built and sustained by modern technology and science, that ceremony stood as a reminder of people and traditions so many pass by. And that has so much to offer.

My reading of nature religions is that their influence is on the rise, particularly in the popular consciousness, probably because of the disconnection that many Americans feel from nature along with a rising awareness and alarm about climate change. Nature religions also appeal to the Spiritual, but Not Religious demographic for these reasons and because they don't really like to use the term "religion" or practice their spirituality in ways that we associate with the term. In this way, they can also deeply connect with the individualizing of the religious search in American culture.[48]

With that in mind, there remains a challenge for natural religions, including Native science (to use Cajete's term) in bringing fundamentally different scientific tools and approaches into a culture in which western science and its technological contributions predominate and have been extraordinarily successful. Who doesn't love their smartphone when lost and seeking direction in an unfamiliar city or modern medical technology in the face of serious injury or illness? Nonetheless, with the upsurge in concern about global climate change, deforestation, extinction, and other forms of environmental degradation, nature religions' engagement with science—which certainly includes its reformulation—will most likely grow in their appeal and influence.

Suggestions for further reading

Since this chapter is wide-ranging, I will suggest more books than the norm, beginning with an eminently approachable introduction to contemporary Paganism: Margo Adler, *Drawing Down the Moon: Witches, Druids, Goddess-Worshippers, and Other Pagans in America* (New York: Penguin, 2006). Two other excellent books on nature religions are Sarah Pike, *New Age and Neopagan Religions in America*, Columbia Contemporary American Religion Series (New York: Columbia University Press, 2006), and Bron Taylor, *Dark Green Religion: Nature Spirituality and the Planetary Future* (Berkeley, CA: University of California, 2009). For native American spiritual traditions, it's hard to beat Vine Deloria for readability and insight, *God Is Red: A Native View of Religion*, 30th Anniversary ed. (Wheat Ridge, CO: Fulcrum, 2003). I also recommend Robin Wall Kimmerer, *Braiding Sweetgrass: Indigenous Wisdom, Scientific Knowledge and the Teachings of Plants* (Minneapolis, MN: Milkweed, 2013). One other well-written introduction is Malcolm Margolin, *The Ohlone Way: Indian Life in the San Francisco-Monterey Bay Area* (Berkeley, CA: Heyday, 1978).

Gregory Cajete blends science and Native American spirituality in *Native Science: Natural Laws of Interdependence* (Santa Fe, NM: Clear Light Publishers, 2000). Many in these religious traditions draw on quantum physics, and though not specifically targeted to nature religions, the classic is Fritjof Capra, *The Tao of Physics: An Exploration of the Parallels Between Modern Physics and Eastern Mysticism*, 5th ed. (Berkeley, CA: Shambala, 2010). More on point is David F. Peat, *Blackfoot Physics: A Journey into the Native American Worldview* (Newburyport, MA: Weiser, 2005).

Notes

1 Molly Hanson, "Could Neo-Paganism Be the New 'Religion' of America?," 30 September 2019, *BigThink*, https://bigthink.com/the-present/modern-paganism, accessed 15 June 2022.
2 Bron Taylor, *Dark Green Religion: Nature Spirituality and the Planetary Future* (Berkeley, CA: University of California, 2009), 5.

3 See Sarah Pike, "Nature Religions and the Spiritualization of Science" Chico State Science and Religions conference, 19 April 2017, https://media.csuchico.edu/media/Nature%20Religions%20and%20the%20Spiritualization%20of%20Science/0_6qv681b3, accessed 15 June 2022.

4 Ibid.

5 "Pagan," *Merriam-Webster Dictionary* online, www.merriam-webster.com/dictionary/pagan, accessed 15 June 2022.

6 *Wikipedia*, "Neopaganism in the United States," https://en.wikipedia.org/wiki/Neopaganism_in_the_United_States, accessed 15 June 2022.

7 U.S. Climate Resilience Toolkit, https://toolkit.climate.gov/topics/tribal-nations, accessed 15 June 2022.

8 John Grim, "Indigenous Lifeways and Knowing the World," in *The Oxford Handbook of Religion and Science*, eds. Clayton et al. (Oxford: Oxford University Press, 2008), 89.

9 See Randy S. Woodley, *Indigenous Theology and the Western Worldview* (Grand Rapids, MI: Baker, 2022), e.g., 44ff.

10 Hanson, "Could Neo-Paganism Be the New 'Religion.'"

11 Pike, "Nature Religions and the Spiritualization of Science."

12 Gregory Cajete, *Native Science: Natural Laws of Interdependence* (Santa Fe, NM: Clear Light Publishers, 2000), 80.

13 See Severin Fowles, *An Archaeology of Doing: Secularism and the Study of Pueblo Religion* (Santa Fe, NM: School for Advanced Research Press, 2013).

14 Cajete, *Native Science*, 14.

15 Sarah Pike, "Nature Religions and the Spiritualization of Science."

16 Grim, "Indigenous Lifeways," in *The Oxford Handbook of Religion and Science*, 88.

17 Cajete, *Native Science*, 5.

18 Ibid., 64.

19 Ibid., 67–71.

20 Cajete begins His talk, "Native Science: The Indigenous Mind Rising," with this point, www.youtube.com/watch?v=3BqoZhp2Zn4, accessed 15 June 2022.

21 Rene Descartes, *Discourse on Method*, Part IV, www.bartleby.com/34/1/6.html, accessed 3 June 2022.

22 Cajete, "Native Science: The Indigenous Mind Rising."

23 Cited in Margot Adler, *Drawing Down the Moon: Witches, Druids, Goddess-Worshippers, and Other Pagans in America* (New York: Penguin, 2006), 399.

24 Ibid., 392–7.

25 "US Climate Resilience Toolkit," https://toolkit.climate.gov/topics/tribal-nations, accessed 15 June 2022.

26 "Guidelines for Considering Traditional Knowledge in Climate Change Initiatives," https://climatetkw.wordpress.com/guidelines, accessed 15 June 2022.

27 See Cajete, "Native Science."

28 Cajete, *Native Science,* 36.

29 Ibid., 74.

30 Ibid., 75.

31 Private email correspondence, May 2022.

32 *The American Yawp Reader*, "Native American Creation Stories," www.americanyawp.com/reader/the-new-world/indian-creation-stories, accessed 18 September 2022.

33 John Alden Mason, *The Ethnology of the Salinan Indians* (Berkeley, CA: University of California Press, 1912), 191–2; https://archive.org/details/ethnologyindians-00masorich, accessed 15 June 2022; W. Powell, *Nineteenth Annual Report of the*

Bureau of American Ethnology to the Secretary of the Smithsonian Institution, 1897–1898, Part I (Washington: The American Yarp Reader website, 1900), 239–40.

34 Robin Wall Kimmerer, *Braiding Sweetgrass: Indigenous Wisdom, Scientific Knowledge, and the Teachings of Plants* (Minneapolis, MN: Milkweed, 2013), 9.

35 Ibid., 7.

36 E.g., Cajete, *Native Science*, 79.

37 Ibid., 269.

38 See "The Role of Eastern Approaches in David Bohm's Scientific-Philosophical Odysseia," 2017, Progress in Biophysics and Molecular Biology, www.researchgate.net/publication/319420494_The_role_of_Eastern_approaches_in_David_Bohm%27s_scientific-philosophical_odysseia, accessed 3 June 2022.

39 Niels Bohr, *Goodreads*, www.goodreads.com/quotes/1293013-physics-is-not-about-how-the-world-is-it-is, accessed 15 June 2022.

40 Robin Collins, "Contributions from the Philosophy of Science," *Oxford Handbook*, eds. Clayton et al., 335.

41 Sable Aradia, "What Is Quantum Woo?" 17 November 2014, *Patheos Blog*, www.patheos.com/blogs/betweentheshadows/2014/11/quantum-woo-what-is-quantum-woo, accessed 15 June 2022.

42 "Quantum Entanglement: A Simple Explanation," www.space.com/31933-quantum-entanglement-action-at-a-distance.html, accessed 11 May 2022.

43 George Musser, "How Einstein Revealed the Universe's Strange "Nonlocality," 1 November 2015, *Scientific American*, www.scientificamerican.com/article/how-einstein-revealed-the-universe-s-strange-nonlocality, accessed 10 May 2022.

44 "Gaia Hypothesis," *Wikipedia*, https://en.wikipedia.org/wiki/Gaia_hypothesis, accessed 15 June 2022.

45 See Pike, "Nature Religions."

46 Cajete, *Native Science*, 36–7.

47 Hanson, "Could Neo-Paganism Be the New 'Religion'?"

48 Catherine L. Albanese, *A Republic of Mind and Spirit: A Cultural History of American Metaphysical Religion* (New Haven, CT: Yale University Press, 2008).

6 Extraordinary influence

Judaism and science

No other religion has as prominent a scientific spokesperson as Albert Einstein—despite his tenuous relationship with traditional elements of Judaism, who can write, "The pursuit of knowledge for its own sake, an almost fanatical love of justice and the desire for personal independence—these are the features of the Jewish tradition which make me thank my stars that I belong to it."[1]

And if Einstein is on target, these features may be why Jews have won 26% of the Nobel Prizes in physics, 28% in medicine, and 19% in Chemistry, yet number about only 0.2% of the world's population. Even more, historian of science Geoffrey Cantor has noted that "by the late 1960s Jews accounted for 17 percent of faculty members of seventeen of the most highly ranked American universities, at a time when Jews constituted 3 percent of the population."[2]

I've commented that Buddhism has an outsized influence on the dialogue of science and religion, but Judaism has even greater direct impact on science. Judaism, the smallest world religion, as the saying goes, punches above its weight. And this fact has led the scholar of Judaism Noah Efron to a striking assertion: "Save Vaudeville and Hollywood, American Jews were nowhere more prominent than in science."[3]

In sum, Jews in the United States have made extraordinary contributions to science, and by and large, find a compatibility of scientific discoveries with their religion. "Apart of some groups of Ultra-Orthodox," according to Cantor's assessment, "Jews have generally been receptive to modern science."[4] All this might make it seem like this chapter will be self-evident. The nature of the Jewish experience, however, brings with it some surprises.

Introducing Judaism: the lightning round Q & A

Once again, here is the now-famous lightning round Q & A. Given the length, it appears that I discovered several critically important points for

DOI: 10.4324/9781003214236-6

understanding Judaism generally before we head into its specific relationship with science.

How many Jews are there?

By far, the smallest religion world religion I am discussing in this book, Judaism has around 15 million followers, about half live in the United States. The size of Judaism greatly affects their relationship with science—more on that later.

What is the problem for which Judaism presents a solution?

In *God is Not One*, Stephen Prothero describes Judaism as "The Way of Exile and Return."[5] In other words, the central problem is exile—we have become distant from God, distant from our community. The solution then is to return, through keeping God's instructions, or law, through storytelling, and through right, ethical action.

Where was Judaism founded?

In the southern Levant, that is, modern-day Israel, Palestine, and Jordan.

How old is it, and does that matter?

This is a religion that's about 4,000 years old. As Arizona State Jewish Studies professor Norbert Samuelson has written, "Since times, places, and peoples constantly change, so do the beliefs expressed in the worshipping community of the Jewish people. Hence, Jewish thought must always be seen as the history of ideas."[6]

Who are founders of Judaism and some key dates?

Around 1800 BCE, God commands Abraham (in the book of Genesis) to go out and bless the world. He is commonly seen as the founder of monotheism (and, for what it's worth, named Ibrahim by Muslims). Moses who gave the Law, or better *Torah*, particularly enshrined in the Ten Commandments around 1250 BCE, as depicted with great fanfare in Exodus 20 and Deuteronomy 5, as well as David, the great King, whose reign was around 1000 BCE. The First Temple was destroyed by the Babylonians in 586 BCE, to be rebuilt under Persian oversight in 515 BCE, and then destroyed by the Romans in 70 CE. Without a temple for . . . animal sacrifice, this created an emergence of the synagogue and rabbinical Judaism.

How about its major branches?

From conservative to liberal, they are Orthodox, Conservative, Reform. The Jewish National Population Survey 2000–2001 found this:

Among American Jews who belong to a synagogue, 39% affiliate with Reform, 33% with Conservative, and 21% with Orthodox with 2% Reconstructionist and 5% "other types." Most American Jews, however, do not belong to any synagogue at all.[7] In addition, many Jews are atheists. All this religious diversity leads Cantor to comment: "Given this diversity of positions, there is no single Jewish perspective on science,"[8] although there are certainly some surprisingly common themes. One of those is an emphasis on *orthopraxis*—right action—over *orthodoxy*—right belief.

Are there shared beliefs with other religions?

Judaism is the monotheistic headwaters for both Christianity and Islam. Samuelson has written about this particularly in relationship, "since Judaism and Christianity share a common textual origin, much of what they believe as least shares common religious terminology."[9]

Are there beliefs particular to Judaism?

As I mentioned earlier with Abraham, but also in relationship with Christians and Muslims, Jews believe in one God, Yahweh (YHVH), who chose the people of Israel and who requires worship, particularly ethical behavior and specific rituals. The ancient Jews recognized several anointed rulers, or messiahs, throughout their history—even Cyrus, the Persian is named "messiah" in Isaiah 45. Jews have traditionally held that a final messiah will come and restore the world.

And practices?

Males are circumcised (the cutting of the foreskin) on the eighth day of life. For males, there's bar mitzvahs at threshold of adulthood, and for Reform Jews, bat mitzvahs for young women. Observant Jews also practice Sabbath weekly from sundown Friday to sundown Saturday.

What are the high holidays?

There are two key high holidays: Yom Kippur (the day of atonement), Rosh Hashanah (literally, the "head of the year" or Jewish New Year). Both are in the fall.

What are its sacred texts?

The Hebrew Bible, essentially the same as the Protestant Old Testament (though ordered differently) is called the Tanakh, which stands for its three parts: *Torah* (Law or instruction), *Nevi'im* (Prophets), and *Ketuvim*

(Writings). But that's not all—the Talmud is a record of the rabbinical oral tradition from several centuries that surround these writings, and it is also sacred. There are actually two—the Palestinian Talmud and the Babylonian from about 350 and 500 CE, respectively. Scholar of Judaism Noah Efron adds that between the Tanakh and the Talmud, "by almost any practical measure the Talmud is the more important of the two."[10]

The scholar for this chapter: Geoffrey Mitelman

Geoffrey Mitelman is director of Sinai and Synapses, a Jewish science and religion organization (full disclosure: where I'm also an advisor). A graduate of both Princeton University and Hebrew Union College-Jewish Institute of Religion, talking with him is always engaging. He's one smart and funny guy, who had a very impressive run on the game show *Jeopardy*. All of this means he often quips with memorable lines like, "The bigger challenge in the Jewish community isn't getting Jews excited about science. It's getting them excited about Judaism."

And with those words, we dive in.

Orthopraxy

To repeat, many have noted that Judaism is a religion of orthopraxis—or right action—much more than orthodoxy—right belief. And so I could say that, in some ways, Judaism is all about ethics. So, let's start here because though Jews differ on matters of belief (which I'll address in a minute), they come together on action. One particular Hebrew phrase stands out, *tikkun olam*, or "the healing of the world." According to a poll by Public Religion Research Institute, "More than 7-in-10 also say that *tikkun olam*, healing the world (72%), and welcoming the stranger (72%) are somewhat or very important values."[11]

The Talmud presents this guideline: "Whoever saves a single life is considered by scripture to have saved the whole world."[12] Similarly, the famous verse from the book of prophet Micah (6:8) reads,

> He has told you, O man, what is good,
> And what the Lord requires of you:
> Only to do justice,
> And to love kindness
> And to walk modestly with your God,
> Then will your name achieve wisdom.
> *(Tanakh Translation*[13]*)*

Though there's much more to say about Jewish ethics, this thread will weave through this chapter because Jews often see their work in science, and the application of science, as intimately connected with ethics.

Formed by history

The key word for this chapter is *extraordinary*. The Jews have an influence beyond a normal reckoning. And the relatively small size of the Jewish population means that their influence on science is noteworthy. Again citing Samuelson, "As a minority, every aspect of its life, including its beliefs, has been influenced both by its own past and the past of its dominant host."[14] It also means that, though we can speak of "Jewish culture" (or cultures), Jews have been dependent on the wider culture in which they are embedded.

Jewish engagement with science can be divided into three periods. The first essentially coincides with the narrative of the Hebrew Bible, and the second continues through the eighteenth century—and though certainly significant—cannot fit within the parameters of this chapter.[15] Within the third period (nineteenth century to the present), leading Jewish scholars Cantor and Mark Swelitz describe the main factors for Jews to embrace science.

> The first is the haskalah, a movement begun by Jewish intellectuals in mid-eighteenth-century Europe inspired by Enlightenment ideals. Maskilim (the followers of the haskalah, the most famous being the German philosopher Moses Mendelssohn [1729–86]) advocated secular studies both as a way to modernize Judaism and as a way to enter mainstream European society.

And

> The second factor was the emancipation of Jews, which started in France in 1791, when they were granted virtually the full rights of citizenship. This created new opportunities for study and work, including participation in fields of science that required university-level education.[16]

One of the Jewish contributions to the history of religion is that to describe a God who acts in and through history. History, conversely, forms the Jewish people.

And this emphasis on history and ethics cannot be divorced from Jewish persecution and especially *antisemitism*. One effect is Jewish migration to the United States. In 1881, the anti-Jewish pogroms in Russia following the assassination of Czar Alexander II resulted in an influx of over 2 million Jews to the United States between 1881 and 1924.[17] These Jews were particularly interested in science because they wanted to assimilate and become integrated into American society. They wanted to become part of the society.

Nevertheless, Nazi Germany's fanatic hatred of Jews, and their expulsion and murder of 6 million Jews in the twentieth century led to their calling the science of Einstein, his theory of relativity, and the work of his colleagues "Jewish physics," which—to the dismay of the German intellectuals of the time—sought "to deprive true physics of 'Arian physics' of its foundations."[18] All this severed the long-standing Jewish contribution to Germany. Thus, Jewish scientists who came to the United States— again, Einstein as a prime example—made enormous contributions to the US science. In fact, a list of displaced German Jewish scientists, as *Physics Today* puts it, represents "a who's who of early 20th-century physics: Hans Bethe, Felix Bloch, Max Born, Albert Einstein, James Franck, Otto Frisch, Fritz London, Lise Meitner, Erwin Schrödinger, Otto Stern, Leo Szilard, Edward Teller, Victor Weisskopf, Eugene Wigner."[19]

Learning through debate

The Jewish tradition emphasizes learning through debate. Mitelman told me that the way of rabbinic thinking is "almost like a peer reviewed paper, where the text becomes like the raw data, which then needs to be interpreted (and potentially challenged)." The Talmud, for example, very rarely says "here's what you should do. The thought process is just as important as the final decision." Menachem Fisch agrees. In his book, *Rational Rabbis: Science and Talmudic Culture*, Fisch argues that modern scientific inquiry and traditional rabbinical inquiry share a common approach— both are highly critical modes of discourse similar to Karl Popper's early-twentieth-century anti-authoritarian philosophy of science.[20]

Part of this tradition of learning and debate is a reasonably flexible approach to sacred scripture. Bar-Ilan University professor Charles Liebman has commented, "Judaism . . . believe[s] in the inerrancy of sacred scripture. But the internal debate centers on the meaning or interpretation of scripture."[21] Arguments about Torah—even argument with God—remains at the center of Jewish identity. This allows almost all Jews the ability not to tend toward the literalist approaches of conservative Christians, which prevents many Jews from certain conflicts with science, like young earth creationism. (More on that later.)

This debate and "peer-review process" seems to connect to the widespread Jewish embrace of science (even if there are various forms of embrace). It's worth citing the former chief rabbi of the United Hebrew Congregations of Great Britain and the Commonwealth Jonathan Sacks, who phrased it this way: most Jews today accept that science and religion both "seek to decode mysteries," but that they are "different intellectual enterprises," one about "explanation" and the other about "interpretation." For them, the "Bible is not proto-science, pseudo-science or myth masquerading as science."[22] In other words, according to Sacks, science and religion fulfill different goals, central to Judaism.

A flexible family

Mitelman told me to keep in mind that Judaism is "a family." And this goes back in some ways to the biblical characters of Abraham and Sarah as a patriarch and matriarch of Judaism. It also means there can be a wide variety, including "Jews of no religion"—they are still part of the family.

The Jewish family has some common traits like freedom of thought and an invitation to family debates. "Get two Jews together," I'm heard from a few sources (and I paraphrase), "and you'll hear at least three opinions." In fact, according to Genesis 32:28 and 35:10, an angel gave the patriarch Jacob the name Israel after they wrestled. The name *Israel*, for the person and the people, means not "the one who finds comfort with God" or "the one who agrees with God," but "the one who *wrestles* with God." This is not a one-off: Moses also argues with God in, for example, Exodus 32. The Jewish tradition is to wrestle with one another and with their God.

And this includes wrestling with various forms of knowledge. In the Q & A, I outlined the various branches of Judaism, and I'd like to put a spotlight on the most influential branch in the United States, Reform Judaism, because of its particular relationship with science. It sees itself as always in process of reforming and is thus always responding to what science has to say. In articulating its eight core tenets in the 1885 Pittsburgh Platform,[23] the sixth reads, "We recognize in Judaism a progressive religion, ever striving to be in accord with the postulates of reason." And this is preceded by the second, which, influenced by the discussions and controversies of evolution states clearly that Judaism is not antagonist to science:

> We recognize in the Bible the record of the consecration of the Jewish people to its mission as the priest of the one God, and value it as the most potent instrument of religious and moral instruction. We hold that the modern discoveries of scientific research in the domain of nature and history are not antagonistic to the doctrines of Judaism, the Bible reflecting the primitive ideas of its own age, and at times clothing its conception of divine Providence and Justice dealing with men in miraculous narratives.[24]

This statement embeds a nuanced approach to scripture. Even more, Reform Jews, like Mitelman, also embody Jewish engagement and collaboration with the insights of science—though, of course, not without argumentation.

The God who creates

Jews are monotheistic—there is one God who is Creator. This does not imply (as it might for some readers) the teaching of *creation out of nothing* (which is much more established in Christianity). *The Jewish Study Bible* renders the first two verses of Genesis as follows: "*¹When* God began to create heaven and earth—²the earth being unformed and void, with darkness over the surface of the deep and a wind form God sweeping over the waters" (emphasis added).[25] According to Mitelman, the Hebrew word in the first verse of Genesis, *bereshit*, is complicated, and probably means "with the beginning."

Creation therefore is more about ordering. Later in Genesis 1:2, the Hebrew *tahowabohu*, translated here "unformed and void" is not tied to creation out of nothing—partly because Jewish scholarship is not as given over to Plato and Aristotle. (Thus Philo, the first century CE Jewish scholar, is much closer to Christianity.) The Harvard biblical scholar Jon D. Levenson's comments in verse 2 summarize this interpretation:

> This clause describes things just before the beginning. To modern people, the opposite of the created order is "nothing," that is, a vacuum. To the ancients, the opposite of the created order was something much worse than "nothing." It was an active malevolent force we can best term "chaos". . . . In the Ancient Near East, however, to say a deity had subdued chaos is to give him the highest praise.[26]

Indeed God continually creates out of chaos. This links evolution and its unfolding creation with the ethics of *tikkun olam*. In other words, by restoring the world, we partner in creation.

Out of this teaching of creation and *tikkun olam*, here are certain characteristically Jewish approaches to the natural world emerges, according to American ethicist and scholar of religion Laurie Zoloth,

> Unlike faith traditions that reify the natural world as essentially sacred and unchangeable, Jewish thought affirms the human ability to alter the natural world, seeing in this alteration the ability to create justice and healing as acts of faith and obligation.[27]

The spectrum of belief among Jewish scientists

Since Judaism is more about orthopraxy over orthodoxy, and since it is first a family and not a system of belief, a stunning variety of ideas about God exist—including "Jews with no religion" with no belief in God. In fact, sociologist of religion and science Elaine Howard Ecklund found that about 75% of Jewish scientists identify as atheists.[28]

I return to great scientists from the Jewish tradition, the atheist Stephen Jay Gould, the proponent of his famous "Non-Overlapping Magisteria" (where science and religion are independent) atheist Stephen Weinberg, the pantheist Albert Einstein, and the orthodox Jews, Gerard Schroeder and Robert Pollack.

Starting with Weinberg, the Nobel-winning physicist not grew up in a broadly Jewish home but abandoned the teachings of his religion, and "became completely unreligious" at the age of 12.[29] Quotations like these two from Weinberg speak for themselves and summarize his position that religion and science are in conflict effectively. "I see no reason to believe what religion teaches because it doesn't fit my scientific picture of the world works. I regard all arguments for the truth of religious teaching as empty and unreliable."[30] And thus, "Religion is an insult to human dignity."[31] Is Weinberg ultimately a Jewish scientist? I include him, minimally because he represents the influence of a leading Jewish thinker on science.

Gould represents a middle group, an independent coexistence position, despite his personal atheism. (This independence model—I somehow feel the need to underline—seems to represent a peace strategy that has not satisfied many.) Gould is a compelling writer, and so it's possible to find captivating examples of his ideas in several locations. I like this one, where he slipped in NOMA effectively in a review of the Intelligent Design leading voice, Philip Johnson's book *Darwin on Trial*. "Science can work only with naturalistic explanations, it can neither affirm no deny other types of actors (like God) in other spheres." He then underlines that Darwin was an agnostic, while his most ardent in the US Asa Gray was a "devout Christian." This leads him to conclude,

> Move on another 50 years to the two greatest evolutionists of our generation G.G. Simpson a humanistic agnostic, Theodosius Dobzhansky, a believing Russian Orthodox. Either half my colleagues are enormously stupid or else Darwinism is fully compatible with religious belief—and equally compatible with atheism, thus proving that the two great realms of nature's factuality and the source of human morality do not strongly overlap.[32]

For the purposes of this chapter, Gould represents one more example of a Jewish atheist scientist, yet one who at least allowed for the religious voices.

I mentioned Einstein both here and at the beginning of this chapter, and he's a fascinating example of one direction that Judaism and science can head. Both Einstein and the seventeenth-century Jewish philosopher Baruch Spinoza (Einstein's intellectual, and particularly philosophical, mentor) rejected a personal God, finding instead a God of the equations, of Deity who created deterministic laws of nature. In his study of the great scientist's life and thought, physicist Max Jammer adds this: "Like Spinoza, Einstein denied the existence of a personal God, modeled after the ideal of a superman as we would say today. In accordance with Jewish thought, both Einstein and Spinoza conceived of an abstract entity in accordance with the biblical 'Thou shalt not make unto thee a graven image or any likeness of any thing' (Exodus 20.4)."[33] Interestingly, the largest percentage of Jews seems to agree with Einstein about God. A Public Religion Research Institute (or PRRI) poll found this: "A plurality (40%) of Jews see God as an impersonal force, compared to 26% who believe God is a person with whom one can have a relationship, and 18% who say they do not believe in God."[34]

Another example is Columbia University professor of biology Robert Pollack, who also directed the Center for the Study of Science and Religion at Columbia University. As Cantor writes, "While he greatly values evolutionary theory for its ability to explain phenomena, he nevertheless recoils from its lack of meaning for our lives."[35] Here, Pollack engages significantly with biological evolution without any ultimate threat to his Jewish beliefs and practices, though he does reject the materialistic threads of Darwin's particular writings.

Gerard Schroeder brings together modern science with a conservative interpretation of Torah. (Other similar voices are Bar-Ilan University physicist Nathan Aviezer and Brooklyn physics teacher Judah Landa.) He received all his degrees from MIT, including his Ph.D. in nuclear physics and earth and planetary sciences. Schroeder finds a reconciliation between the 6-day creation, as Genesis describes it, with the scientific evidence that the world is around 14 billion years old. He employs the concept of the *perceived* flow of time for a given space–time event in an expanding universe varies with the observer's *perspective* of that same event. Using Einstein's general relativity, he calculates the effect of the stretching of space–time. From the perspective of the point of origin (or $t = 0$) of the Big Bang, Einstein's equations present a time dilates by a factor of roughly 1,000,000,000,000. This means that one trillion days on earth would appear to pass as one day from that point. Applying this method to the estimated age of the universe of the order of 13.7 billion years, and from the perspective of the point of origin, our universe would then appear to be in the initial stage of its sixth day.[36]

Just to be sure I haven't lost the point of these examples: these scientists, despite the wide variety of their views, are all Jewish in some way.

The particular case of evolution

One particularly significant topic is evolution—and as I've stated in my chapter on Christianity, many in my college classes simply set out the dichotomy: God or evolution. They seem to have been schooled by Christian fundamentalists. In contrast, over 80% of Jews accept evolution,[37] which contrasts markedly with recalcitrant anti-evolutionary Christian fundamentalism. Cantor has written, "Although a number of Jews have been opposed to Darwin's theory, there has been no virulent anti-evolutionist movement among Jews comparable with the very hostile creationist opposition by some Christians and Muslims."[38]

Similarly, there is no robust tradition of 6-day creationism in Judaism. Already in the fourteenth century, Rabbi Bachya ben Asher wrote about the six "days" in Genesis 1,

> For those days were not like human days, but they were the days from which one formed the unfathomable years, in a similar sense to the verse (Job 36:26): "Behold God is mighty beyond our knowledge; the number of his years is unfathomable."[39]

As a rule, the more conservative one is religious, the more resistant to evolution. By analogy, let's take on the hardest case—the most conservative form of Judaism. In the 1990s, a young ultra-Orthodox rabbi, Nosson Slitkin, began publishing a series of popular books that presented an integration of zoology using modern science, generally speaking, within traditional Jewish framework. At first, Slitkin's ideas and books were well received by all segments of Orthodoxy, including the ultra-Orthodox. But in September 2004, some leading ultra-Orthodox rabbis condemned his writings as heretical, and their criticisms included his support for evolution and the age of the earth. Slitkin asserted that he was faithful to traditional sources for Orthodoxy like Samson Raphael Hirsch (1808–1888) and Abraham Isaac Kook (1865–1935). It seems that these particular connections with Jewish tradition didn't matter. Swetlitz and Cantor write, "These reactions to Slitkin's writings also reflect internal divisions within ultra-Orthodoxy over how to respond to the challenge of modernity."[40] Science reflects cultural ideas and not simply facts.

This case is fascinating as a representative of the end of the Jewish spectrum of opinion on human evolution. But even then, it's not universal for Jewish Orthodoxy. The Rabbinical Council of America (RCA), one of the world's largest organizations of Orthodox rabbis, has stated that "evolutionary theory, properly understood, is not incompatible with belief in a Divine Creator, nor with the first 2 chapters of Genesis."[41]

With that said, there are a few places where biological evolution and/or Darwinism (those terms are slightly different since evolution has, well, evolved since Darwin) meets up with some significant flashpoints in Judaism.

Specifically, it is also notable that hatred of Jews, specifically antisemitism, was originally linked with Darwin's theory. As Cantor and Swetlitz write, there was "the use of evolution in racial theory in Germany in order to provide 'scientific' credence to anti-Semitism."[42] And they continue by noting its source,

> The term "anti-Semitism" had been coined in 1879 by Wilhelm Marr (1819–1904) in his book *Der Sieg des Judenthums über das Germanenthum* (The Triumph of the Jews over the Germans). Marr alluded to the notion, prevalent after Darwin published his theory, that material evolution applied to human species. Accordingly, differences between peoples and their social characteristics had been shaped by natural selection. Marr's book was a deliberate attempt to show that discrimination against the Jews was based on "scientific" anthropological foundations: they were an alien Volk or nation.[43]

Even with this connection, generally Jews accepted evolution, though this is not entirely universal.

There is certainly more to Jewish history than the Old Testament and the Holocaust (also called *Shoah*, Hebrew for "catastrophe"), which I've tried to demonstrate in this chapter. Still, the Holocaust looms large, and the murder of European Jews had both direct and indirect effects on Jewish responses to evolution. To quote Cantor and Swetlitz once again,

> The concept of "race" became discredited among biologists and social scientists—Jews playing leading roles in that effort-and social and cultural explanations became prominent in the social sciences, where Jews continued to work in large numbers. Interest in human heredity continued, using new tools in human and population genetics. In Israel this research was part of an ongoing public debate, stimulated by the influx of immigrants from many countries, about the origin of the Jewish people.[44]

As I commented earlier, the United States (and Israel) subsequently emerged as the leading centers for Jewish thought and life. It also meant that most rabbis and theologians focused on other issues, such as Jewish belief post-Holocaust and the State of Israel. They "paid little attention to science, including evolution, except for the issues raised by biomedical ethics. Only in the last decade of the twentieth century did some rabbis and Jewish intellectuals rekindle an interest in Judaism's relationship to science, including evolution."[45]

Technology and Judaism

I mentioned earlier that we cannot understand Judaism without grasping its status as a minority religion and culture. And this helps us comprehend Jewish responses to various forms of technology. Samuelson has commented that because the population of Jews today after the Holocaust (especially European Jews) is small, "there are some genetic diseases to which Jews are especially prone."[46] They represent in biological terms, a "breeding population" (a population within which free interbreeding takes place and evolutionary change may appear and be preserved).[47] And thus Jews have embraced modern genetic as well as reproductive technologies.

Another angle on technology is transhumanism, which exploits technology so that humans can transcend the limitations of biologically based life. Like many Jewish perspectives, there is diversity. I offer two representative responses.

Hava Tirosh-Samuelson, Professor of Modern Judaism and Director of Jewish Studies at Arizona State University, has commented that the overall Jewish response to this movement is negative.[48] She offers three reasons: "First, transhumanism aggrandizes the human and aspires to deification of the human." Second, it's "techno-idolatry. Idolatry? Yes, "precisely because it venerates human-made inventions and the people who create them . . . Third, because of its valorization of technology, transhumanism considers the biological human but an early and flawed phase of the human species."

Not every Jewish leading voice would concur (which she affirms), but hers is an influential one. Still, Rabbi Ira Bedzow, director of the Biomedical Ethics and Humanities Program at New York Medical College, says that human enhancement can be useful within limits. He draws on Jewish interpretation of the Bible—a "midrash"—that is favorable toward improving creation, as long as the purpose is moral.

A wicked Roman provocateur asks Rabbi Akiva whether the works of God are greater or the works of man. Akiva surprised him by saying the works of man, and brings him some ears of corn along with some cakes. "The former are the works of God, the latter of man. Are not the latter superior to the ears of corn?" So too with circumcision, says Akiva. If God hadn't wanted Jews to perform circumcision, God would have created babies that were born circumcised, "but the Holy One blessed be He has given the commandments for the sole purpose of refining our character through them.[49]

And here again, in this specific Jewish response to transhumanism, the themes of *tikkun olam* and orthopraxis reappear.

I'll close this with two brief additional comments. Like any religion after the COVID-19 pandemic outbreak of 2020, Jews have utilized technology to expand their worship presence. I often direct my students in the Northern California city of Chico to participate virtually in the sabbath service at Central Synagogue in New York City. Technology reaches across the country. But Jewish law also provides tethers on technology, particularly the central Jewish practice of sabbath or rest. Limiting technology, as a sabbath practice is a particular insight from Judaism. "Tech sabbath"[50] is one example—where cell phones put away from sundown Friday through sundown Saturday. Similarly, I participated in the Enhancing Life Project, where several scholars researched means of human flourishing. One project by Hebrew University Professor of Communications Menahem Blondheim[51] researched the psychological effects of teens were given a 2-week break from their cell phones. He found that they almost universally experienced higher levels of happiness and lower levels of stress. This to my ears was the essence of a tech sabbath.

Final thoughts

It's hard for me to imagine anything for Judaism except a continued strong influence in science and technology. That seems settled, but the question—following Mitelman's quip with which I began—remains as to whether Jews continue to hold to their traditional beliefs. Put another way, in the pairing "Judaism and science," the latter term seems quite secure, but the former seems more in jeopardy as the actual number of Jews decreases in the United States while Jewish secularism is on the rise.

This chapter started with an epitaph from the nontraditional Jew, Einstein. Let's return to him by way of the Dartmouth College physicist and astronomer Marcelo Gleiser who summarized how Einstein's insights are sources of continued inspiration.

I thought of Einstein and his belief that scientific enterprise is the only true religion. He meant it in a deeply spiritual way, seeing science as an act of devotion. Scientists should engage with the mystery of existence, inspired by a deep sense of awe and filled with humility. If science is seen this way, many more will be ready to embrace it as one of the highest expressions of the human spirit.[52]

One can hope—or at least I do—that Judaism, which Einstein credited for his scientific thinking and his ethics, can thereby continue to bring about the healing of the world.

Suggestions for further readings

There are several excellent options for understanding Judaism and science. A good place to begin is by grasping Jewish biblically scholarship through *The Jewish Study Bible*, edited by Adele Berlin and Marc Zvi Brettler (Oxford: Oxford University Press, 2004); this brings together leading Jewish biblical scholars. For a historical approach, see Noah Efron, *Judaism and Science: A Historical Introduction* (Westport, CT: Greenwood, 2006). Throughout this chapter, I drew on collection of essays on evolution edited by Geoffrey Cantor and Marc Swetlitz, *Jewish Tradition and the Challenge of Darwinism* (Chicago, IL: University of Chicago Press, 2006), as well as that very famous scientist—so famous we refer to him by last name only, Einstein: Max Jammer, *Einstein and Religion: Physics and Theology* (Princeton, NJ: Princeton University Press, 1999). There are several relevant chapters you'll find in the footnotes. Still, I'll highlight the excellent summary by Norbert Samuelson, "Judaism and Science," in *The Oxford Handbook of Religion and Science*, eds. Philip Clayton and Zachary Simpson (Oxford: Oxford University Press, 2006).

Notes

1 Einstein, *Ideas and Opinions*, 3rd ed. (New York: Crown, 1995), 185.
2 Geoffrey Cantor, "Modern Judaism," in *Science and Religion Around the World,* eds. John Hedley Brooke and Ron Numbers (Oxford: Oxford University Press), 59.
3 Noah Efron, *Judaism and Science: A Historical Introduction* (Westport, CT: Greenwood, 2006), 178.
4 Cantor, "Modern Judaism," 62.
5 Stephen Prothero, *God Is Not One: The Eight Rival Religions That Run the World* (New York: HarperOne, 2010), ch. 7.
6 Norbert Samuelson, "Judaism and Science," in *The Oxford Handbook of Religion and Science*, eds. Philip Clayton and Zachary Simpson (Oxford: Oxford University Press, 2006), 41.
7 "The Jewish National Population Survey 2000–2001," https://cdn.fedweb.org/fed-34/136/National-Jewish-Population-Study.pdf, accessed 16 June 2022.
8 Cantor, "Modern Judaism," 45.

9 Samuelson, "Judaism and Science," 41.
10 Noah Efron, "Early Judaism," in *Science and Religion around the World*, eds. Brooke and Numbers, 23.
11 "Chosen for What? Jewish Values in 2012," www.prri.org/research/jewish-values-in-2012, accessed 16 June 2022.
12 Sanhedrin 37a.
13 Adele Berlin and Marc Zvi Brettler, eds., *The Jewish Study Bible* (Oxford: Oxford University Press, 2004).
14 Samuelson, "Judaism and Science," 41.
15 See ibid., 42.
16 Cantor and Swetliz, *Jewish Tradition and the Challenge of Darwinism* (Chicago, IL and London: University of Chicago Press, 2006), 10.
17 Cantor, "Modern Judaism," 57.
18 Jammer, *Einstein and Religion: Physics and Theology* (Princeton, NJ: Princeton University Press, 1999), 59.
19 "The Scientific Exodus from Nazi Germany," 26 September 2018, *Physics Today*, https://physicstoday.scitation.org/do/10.1063/PT.6.4.20180926a/full, accessed 16 June 2022.
20 Cantor, "Modern Judaism," 62.
21 Charles S. Liebman, *Deceptive Images: Toward a Redefinition of American Judaism* (New Brunswick, NJ: Transaction Books, 1988), 44.
22 Jonathan Sacks, *The Great Partnership: Science, Religion, and the Search for Meaning* (New York: Schocken, 2014), 284–5.
23 "The Pittsburgh Platform, 1885," www.myjewishlearning.com/article/the-pittsburgh-platform-1885, accessed 16 June 2022.
24 Ibid.
25 *The Jewish Study Bible.*
26 Levenson in *The Jewish Study Bible*, 13.
27 Judaism Zoloth, "Contemporary Issues in Science and Religion," in *Encyclopedia of Science and Religion*, ed. Wentzel Vrede van Huyssteen (New York: Macmillan, 2003), 483.
28 Elaine Howard Ecklund, *Science vs. Religion: What Scientists Really Think* (Oxford: Oxford University Press, 2010), 32–6.
29 Weinberg in Steve Paulson, *Atoms and Eden: Conversations on Religion and Science* (Oxford: Oxford University Press, 2010), 261.
30 Ibid.
31 Quoted in Brooke and Numbers, 60.
32 Stephen J. Gould, "Impeaching a Self-Appointed Judge," review of Philip Johnson's *Darwin on Trial, Scientific American* 267 (1992): 118–21, https://www.jstor.org/stable/24939153, accessed 19 September 2022.
33 Jammer, 47.
34 "Chosen for What? Jewish Values in 2012," www.prri.org/research/jewish-values-in-2012, accessed 11 May 2022.
35 Cantor, "Modern Judaism," 54.
36 Schroeder, "The Age of the Universe: One Reality Viewed From Two Different Perspectives," 3 October 2019, https://aish.com/the-age-of-the-universe-one-reality-viewed-from-two-different-perspectives, accessed 16 June 2022.
37 "2014 Pew Religious Landscape Study," www.pewresearch.org/religion/religious-landscape-study/religious-tradition/jewish/views-about-human-evolution, accessed 6 June 2022.

38 Cantor, "Modern Judaism," 55.

39 See Jammer, *Einstein and Science*, 197.

40 Cantor and Swetlitz, 16–7.

41 "Creation, Evolution, and Intelligent Design," 27 December 2005, *RCA*, https://web.archive.org/web/20120503235604/www.rabbis.org/news/article.cfm?id=100635, accessed 6 June 2022.

42 Ibid., 6.

43 Raphael Falk, "Zionism, Race, and Eugenics," in *Jewish Tradition and the Challenge of Darwinism* (Chicago, IL: University of Chicago Press, 2006), 140; citing Wilhelm Marr, *Der Sieg des] udenthums uber das Germanenthum: Yom nicht confessionellen Standpunkt aus Betrachtet* (Bern: Rudolf Constable, 1879).

44 Cantor and Swetlitz, 15.

45 Ibid., 15.

46 Samuelson, 51.

47 "Breeding Population," *Meriam-Webster Dictionary* online, www.merriam-webster.com/dictionary/breeding%20population, accessed 16 June 2022.

48 "Religious Transhumanism? Jewish Transhumanism? No!" www.patheos.com/blogs/publictheology/2022/03/religious-transhumanism-6-jewish-no, accessed 16 June 2022.

49 Simona Weinglass, "The Cyborg Revolution Is Here. Is It Good for the Jews?," 1 October 2015, *The Times of Israel*, www.timesofisrael.com/the-cyborg-revolution-is-here-is-it-good-for-the-jews, accessed 16 June 2022.

50 Tiffany Shlain, "Tech's Best Feature: The Off Switch," 1 March 2013, https://hbr.org/2013/03/techs-best-feature-the-off-swi, accessed 6 June 2022.

51 See http://enhancinglife.uchicago.edu/people/menahem-blondheim, accessed 16 June 2022.

52 Gleiser, "Science vs. God: Understanding Reality Is Not a Battle Between Reason and Faith," 6 April 2022, *Big Think*, https://bigthink.com/13-8/science-god-false-choice/?fbclid=IwAR0ZrgAq73_m_iMC-iMoLN4PdxjwcK-q5cC68jCJzElK_P4EdEFDglTxwZjU, accessed 16 June 2022.

7 Creation and the oneness of God

Islam and science

I could say that all the monotheistic faiths—which comprise the bulk of religious people worldwide—have similar approaches to science and technology. At least, it's a useful generalization. And though Islam builds its vision of science from the Quran, which is not a part of the Jewish and Christian sacred texts, the three share insights and family resemblances. In this chapter, this is why you'll hear similar melodies from the other two faiths, but in a slightly different key.

In a certain way, Muslims encounter science repeatedly in their practice, whether they live in Jakarta, Medina, Gaza City, or Dearborn, Michigan (home to the largest Muslim population per capita in the United States) because they need to know where Mecca is. As Islamic Studies scholar Ahmad Dallal writes, "Muslims are enjoined to face Mecca during their five daily prayers, just as all mosques are supposed to be oriented toward the Kaaba in Mecca, in what is known as the direction of the *qibla*."[1] (Muslims use this in a variety of practices, particularly the direction of prayer.) And thus, the science of astronomy (alongside other sciences) directly connects with daily Islamic practice.

With that said, it seems that Islam and science are not at odds. "Most Muslims," according to a Pew Research Center, "do not believe there is an inherent tension between religion and science."[2] Nonetheless, as I'll note later, there is also a prevalent Muslim resistance to biological evolution. In addition, when we realize that the western world—aka Europeans and Americans—have set the definition for "modern science," which historically has been often happened simultaneously while colonizing Muslim-majority countries, it makes sense that the relationship between Islam and modern science is both tensive and fascinating.

And what is most interesting can only be found in the details.

DOI: 10.4324/9781003214236-7

Introducing Islam: the lightning round Q & A

Many Americans have a distorted view of Islam (sadly too often associating it with terrorism), and so let's set the scene with some general questions.

What does the word "Islam" mean?

It is Arabic for "submission" (that leads to) "peace." The word is related etymologically to Arabic *salaam*—as in the greeting *as-salaam-alaikum*, "peace to you"—as well as the well-known Hebrew word for peace *shalom*. And, on a related note, a *Muslim* is one who submits to God and finds peace.

What is the problem for which Islam presents a solution?

The problem that Islam wants to solve is pride and ingratitude for God that adds up to the sense that we can get along on our own without God. The solution is submission to God, partly through the practices described later.

How many Muslims are there in the world?

1.8 billion in the world with about three and half million in the United States. This implies that there is dazzling diversity. Columbia University Professor Edward Said has written that we might do better to speak of "Islams rather than Islam." And he added,

> once one gets a tiny step beyond core beliefs (since even those are very hard to reduce to a simple set of doctrinal rules) and the centrality of the Koran [Quran], one has entered an astoundingly complicated world whose enormous—one might even say unthinkable—collective history alone has yet to be written.[3]

Where and when was Islam founded?

The Arabian Peninsula, especially in the key cities of Medina (the first Muslim city) and Medina (the city of the Muslim Prophet Muhammad). Muslims start their calendar with the year 1, or 622 CE in the Gregorian Calendar, when Medina adopted the religion proclaimed by Muhammed.

Tell more about that founder.

His full name is Muhammad ibn Abdullah, and he lived between 570 and 632 CE. (By extension, this makes Islam, one of the newer religions in this book.)

What are the major branches of Islam?

Put simply, and therefore with some distortion, the largest percentage worldwide are Sunnis at about 85%, who are spread throughout the globe, and the Shiites, at approximately 15%, who are mainly around Iran. Both are present in the United States. There is a mystical strand of Islam, Sufism, which can be found in either.

By the way, are most Muslims Arab?

There are certainly many Muslims that speak Arabic in the Middle East, but they are only a minority. Most Muslims live in Asia. And the country that has the highest percentage of Muslims is Indonesia at something like 87%, and they have three times as many as Saudi Arabia, Afghanistan, and Iraq combined.[4]

What are some key beliefs and practices?

The Oxford Dictionary of Islam writes, "Tawhid is the defining doctrine of Islam—the unity and uniqueness of God as creator and sustainer of the universe."[5] *Allah* is God in Arabic but is not a name specific to Islam. Arabic-speaking Christians use Allah as well. In addition, Muslims hold to the conviction that the same God is revealed (imperfectly) in the Jewish and Christian Bibles. And then there are mosque services on Fridays, ablutions (washing with water) before prayer, and no consumption of alcohol or pork, as well as the Five Pillars of Islam: Confession of Faith, Daily Prayer, Giving Alms, Pilgrimage to Mecca once in a Muslim's life, and Fasting during the season of Ramadan.

Any key texts?

The supreme and final book for Muslims is the Quran, which Muslims believe record the very speech of God (spoken in Arabic), revealed to Muhammad 610–632 CE. In addition, there's the hadith, which are records of Muhammad's sayings and acts.

Yunus Dogan Telliel and Nidhal Guessoum accompany us

To learn more, I discussed Islam with Yunus Dogan Telliel, a Muslim scholar of rhetoric and anthropology at Worcester Polytechnic Institute. He's a friend and colleague on the leadership team from the Science, Technology, and Religion group (or "program unit") of the American, Academy of Religion, and he's just a great person to talk with—every time I do, I leave with fresh insights. In this case, he helped me to grasp the rhetorical and cultural angle on Islam and science (perspectives I've tried to bring to other chapters as well). I also emailed Algerian-born astrophysicist Nidhal Guessoum, a leading thinker in Islam views on science, and I integrate his responses later.

History matters then and now

I've tried to keep the recounting of the history to a minimum for any of these religions, but to grasp Islam's current relationship with science, understanding the past is essential.

Few people in the United States know about the golden period of Islamic science from the eighth to thirteenth centuries, which represents a flowering of mathematics, experimental science. But we do know key scientific terms like *algebra, algorithm, alkaline,* and they all have Arabic roots (*al* means "the" in Arabic) that emerged during this period. The Muslim world engaged (and preserved) the works of Aristotle for science and philosophy, particularly in the writings of Andalusian polymath and jurist Averroes (which is the Latinized version of Ibn Rushd) during the flowering of interfaith life of twelfth-century Spain. During this period, it is worth noting that the motivation for a Muslim pursuit of mathematics was motivated to a large degree by the desire to accurately position mosques in the orientation of prayer toward the Kaaba in Mecca.

The destruction of Istanbul Observatory in 1580 provides one coda to the decline of science in Islamic culture. And gradually, European science began ascending on the heels of this descent. As often happens, this took center stage in warfare. Historian of Islam Daniel Brown writes, "The Ottoman army was driven back from Vienna in 1683 in a decisive enough way to show that it was falling behind European armies in technology and tactics."[6] There are a variety of factors, and it is relevant and worth underlining that the Muslim world is not by nature against science. As Dallal writes, "the decline of the rational sciences in the Muslim world, along with other intellectual activities, was a symptom of complex and historically specific social, political, and economic factors and not the result of an inevitable unfolding of culture."[7] Historically, this also means that what we define as modern science is European. Thus, many Muslims resist the idea that this epitomizes the only form of science. Iranian philosopher and University Professor of Islamic studies at George Washington University Seyyed Hossein Nasr, for example, highlights the Importance of developing an "Islamic Science,"[8] one grounded in Islamic thought. We return to this theme throughout, and I will specifically cite Nasr later.

Now I turn to Guessoum. He presents a non-literal and "multilevel reading of the Quran"[9] that will assist Muslims in engaging modern science.[10] In responding to a question that asked about his assessment of "science in the Islamic world today" offered this,

> It's abysmal by all kinds of measures: how many books and publications are written or translated in the Muslim word, how many patents come from Muslim inventors, how Muslim students are performing in the international arena. By all these measures, the Muslim world is way, way down.[11]

Guessoum notes that most of the Muslim world was under colonial rule for quite some time, where the rate of literacy is often less than 10%. But he adds this: "We can blame colonialism for only so much." He instead points to "versions of Islam that impose strict readings of Scripture . . . . If any religion, including Islam, denies the spirit of free inquiry, people can't investigate and write what they want to write. That's the end of science."[12] And that leads to rejecting evolution.

Of course, let me be quick to add that not all is grim, and not all leading Muslim science is in the past. There are many contemporary prominent Muslim scientists, and it's worth noting that two Muslims have won Nobel Prizes in science: Mohammad Abdus Salam (Physics, 1979) and Ahmed Zewail and Aziz Sancar (Chemistry, 1999 and 2015, respectively).

Key terms and natural theology

How does Islam approach *science* and *religion*? Let's start with vocabulary. Key is the Arabic word *ilm*. Telliel told me that it is the broadest word for "knowledge" and one of the most frequent words in the Quran, used over 780 times.[13] It came to mean "science" (that is, the systematization of facts), as well as "revealed knowledge," that is, the scriptures specifically and religious knowledge more generally.[14] Today, when we think of science, we hardly ever include those later categories. In addition, we also must include the Arabic words *hikma* "suprarational means" and *maarifa* "knowledge" (matters of fact). Once again, none of these exactly map onto the word science.

I realize I've finished the lightning round Q & A, but I still have one more key question: Is there a natural theology in Islam? By this term, I mean this: Can human beings find a knowledge of God outside God's own revelation? The answer, strictly speaking, has almost universally been No. Muslim tradition does highlight that natural phenomena in their beauty and constancy point to God, but also that natural cause and effect cannot be fully understood without God. Al-Ghazali (1058–1111), in his influential book, *Moderation of Faith* declared that God *directly* causes all events and entities:

> You have known from the sum of this that all temporal events, their substances and accidents, those occurring in the entities of the animate and the inanimate, come about through the power of God, may he be exalted. He alone holds the sole prerogative of inventing them. No created thing comes about through another created thing. Rather, all come about through divine power.[15]

In his view, God is the cause of all, which can restrict the ability to study natural causes, the basis of modern science as we know it.

This is a version of *occasionalism*—again I lean on the *Oxford Dictionary of Islam*—

> events are the result of entities whose cause is God alone. . . . A human agent is properly said to be able to act only at the moment he or she actually performs the action; only at this instant [or occasion] does God create in the person the ability to perform it.[16]

A commitment to occasionalism means there is ultimately no natural or secondary causation (with God as the First Cause). Ultimately, then this teaching contracts the modern scientific consensus of methodological naturalism—that science limits itself to *natural* (and not supernatural) cause and effect. As Oxford professor of science and religion Alister McGrath comments, this teaching "led to the marginalization of the notion of causality within the natural world, which was increasingly becoming the object of study by the natural sciences."[17]

Naturally, many leading Muslim scientists, working in modern research universities and elsewhere, operate under the guidelines of methodological naturalism. Many are devout, traditional Muslims. Others take a different path. At any interreligious conference I attended a few years ago, I met a scholar who had no qualms about calling himself Muslim and who also concluded from his work as a scientist, that he was deist. Because of the inexorable and interlocking laws of nature, there was no reason to conclude that God could work outside of those laws. He and Albert Einstein would agree (as I note in the chapter on Judaism).

The Quran and science

Let's move to the single most important source for Muslim approaches to science, the Quran: There is of course more to Islam than the Quran, and yet, the Muslim Holy Book is so central it's impossible to understand Islam and science without highlighting the Quran. I begin with two longer quotations to set the context.

The scholar of religion Huston Smith has written in *The World's Religions*,

> If signs be sought, let them be not of Muhammad's greatness but of God's, and for these one need only open one's eyes. The heavenly bodies holding their swift, silent course in the vault of heaven, the incredible order of the universe, the rain that falls the relieve the parched earth, palms bending with golden fruit, ships that glide across the seas laden with goodness—can this be the handiwork of gods of stone? What fools to cry for signs when creation tokens nothing else! In an age of credulity, Muhammad taught respect for the world's incontrovertible order, a respect that was to bring Muslims to science before it did Christians.[18]

This is a stunning overview by a leading scholar. It finds resonance with what Pakistani-Canadian Islamic scholar Muzaffar Iqbal presents in his essay for *The Study Quran*,

> Built into the Quranic description of the cosmos is a teleology that anchors the physical cosmos in a metaphysical realm, thereby establishing an incontrovertible nexus between God and the cosmos, on the other hand, and whatever exists in the cosmos and its raison d'être, on the other . . . anchoring of the physical cosmos and all that exists in it in a realm beyond the physical is utterly lost in modern science.[19]

There is thus a deep connection between the Quran and the study of nature that is the essence of science. And there is a debate about whether it can be modern science, as I've presented in this book, which is defined by methodological naturalism.

Telliel, who has a particular sensitivity to the rhetorical structure of this encounter of Islam and science, reminded me of the theme of a changing vocabulary for "science." What emerged in Christian Europe in the sixteenth and seventeenth centuries "generated a discourse that became universal and secularized." And so we arrive at a key question, "Who counts as modern and as civilized? We need to be a conceptual reshuffling. And this leads to a way of thinking about knowledge and the ends and means of knowledge," which really is why the conversation about science and religion raises so many key cultural issues.

At any rate, the question of how well modern science fits with the Quran specifically and Islam generally is paralleled in the argument by Nasr—incidentally, trained at a temple to western science, MIT—there is "an Islamic alternative to Western science."[20] Essentially, the problem is that science, as it's often defined, is indelibly marked with western and Enlightenment concepts, but even more, assumptions. As he writes in *The Oxford Handbook of Religion and Science*, "there is the most essential criticism concerning the at best neutral attitude of modern science concerning religion and the paramount role of science in creating a mental ambiance from which God and the eschatological [end of time] realities are absent and, therefore, finally 'unreal.'"[21] This approach and the "ambience" it creates are antithetical to Muslims' view of the reality and truth. He continues with a rhetorical question, "How can Islam accept any form of knowledge that is not rooted in God and does not necessarily lead to Him?"[22] This seems impossible to affirm for Nasr who writes,

> In conclusion, it is necessary to repeat that any science that could legitimately be called Islamic science, and not be disruptive of the whole Islamic order, must be one that remains aware of the "vertical cause" of all things, along with the horizontal, a science that issues from and returns to the Real (*al-Haqa*).[23]

At the same time, Guessoum calls this approach in which the Sunna or prophet tradition is "Sacred Science" (or *scientia sacra*) simply "erroneous."[24] Nasr's concern about methodological naturalism as philosophical naturalism is misguided according to Guessoum, who sees a reasonably clear distinction between religion and science when he comments on the limitations of *sacra scientia*,

> In my view, what we have here is a mixing of two domains, the area of rigorous, universal, empirical methodology for the exploration and investigation of nature and the cosmos, and the area of finding meaning in what we discover and learn. The two are primarily different in that the first one is objective while the second is subjective, and they have fundamentally different approaches. Mixing them simply leads to utter confusion. Moreover, whatever one does about meaning, purpose, and adding spiritual considerations, cannot come at the cost of sacrificing large swaths of established science, as Nasr and his followers do by rejecting the Big Bang cosmology and evolutionary biology.[25]

If it sounds to you like this is the independence model of religion and science against a conflict model, our ears are hearing the same things. And if it reminds us that there is significant diversity within Islam about how to approach science, then we are on the right track.

The Quran and creation

One of the key beliefs of Islam, like Judaism and Christianity, is that God creates. The Quran has several passages that highlight God's creation of the natural world. Though this is a bit longer than most of quotations from sacred writings in this book, I think it's worth the space and attention to quote Surah (or chapter) 15:19–31:

> We spread the earth, and placed stabilizers in it, and in it We grew all things in proper measure. And in it We created livelihoods for you, and for those for whom you are not the providers. There is not a thing but with Us are its stores, and We send it down only in precise measure. We send the fertilizing winds; and send down water from the sky, and give it to you to drink, and you are not the ones who store it. It is We who give life and cause death, and We are the Inheritors. And We know those of you who go forward, and We know those who lag behind. It is your Lord who will gather them together. He is the Wise, the Knowing. We created the human being from clay, from molded mud. And the jinn We created before, from piercing fire. Your Lord said to the angels, "I am creating a human being from clay, from molded mud. When I have formed him, and breathed into him of My spirit, fall down prostrating before him." So the angels prostrated themselves, all together. Except for Satan. He refused to be among those who prostrated themselves.[26]

In addition, the Quran (13:16) affirms that God created everything: "God is the Creator of all things, and He is the One, the Paramount [or Omnipotent]." The implication is clear—all things depend on God who sustains them—which the Quran clearly expresses, "O mankind! You are needful of God: and He is the Self-Sufficient, the Praised" (33:15).

From these verses, Muslim scholars have developed the Kalam cosmological argument with great sophistication—that the existence of a creation requires a Creator. This is an argument or even proof that has traction today and that possesses a venerable pedigree. The medieval philosopher Al-Ghazali wrote, "Every being which begins has a cause for its beginning; now the world is a being which begins; therefore, it possesses a cause for its beginning."[27] This argument more recently has been connected with creations having a beginning point through Big Bang cosmology, which is a key component of contemporary formulations of the Kalam argument. Naturally, like all arguments for God, it has its proponents and detractors today.

Modern science depicts an evolving and dynamic universe, and so a key issue is whether God created once in the past or is continuously creating. Scholars have interpreted two Quranic verses to support this view: "Those in the heavens and on the earth entreat Him: every day He is upon a task" (55:29) and "Did We weary in the first creation? Nay, but they are in doubt regarding a new [or fresh] creation" (50:15).

Indeed, modern science also points to a vastness beyond the Earth. Modern astronomy has discovered thousands of exoplanets, or planets outside our solar system, and with this comes the possibility of intelligent extraterrestrial life. Muslim scholars point to the ascription to God that begins in the Quran (1:2–3), especially the second part: "In the Name of God, the Compassionate, the Merciful. Praise to God, Lord of the worlds." Two have found additional Quranic evidence for the vastness of God's creation beyond our terrestrial sphere. Imam Muhammad al-Baqhir has written, "Maybe you see that God created only this single world and that God did not create Homo sapiens besides you. Well, I swear by God that God indeed created thousands and thousands of worlds and thousands and thousands of humankind." Muslim theologian and philosopher Fakhr al-Din al-Razr offers this as a commentary on the Quran:

> God, the Exalted is capable of actualizing all possibilities. Thus, be He Exalted is capable of creating thousands upon thousands of worlds beyond this world, each of which would be greater and more massive than this world . . . and the argument of the philosophers for the uniqueness of this world is weak and poor, being based on invalid premises.[28]

The particular case of scientific *tafsir*

One of the key topics of science and Islam is "the scientific miracle (*ijaz*) of the Qur'ān."[29] By some reckonings, there are 750 "scientific verses" in the Quran that contain facts and theories later discovered by modern science.[30] The specific name for this is "scientific *tafsir*." And *tafsir* can be translated reasonably well as "interpretation." As Guessoum describes the argument, many Quranic verses and hadith "if read and interpreted 'scientifically,' express in semi-explicit ways scientific truth that were only discovered recently."[31] Full disclosure: Guessom presents his book *The Young Muslim's Guide to Modern Science* as an antidote to this thinking.[32]

Related to the Quran and science is the influential work by Ottoman grand vizier and astronomer Gazi Ahmed Muhtar Pasha (1839–1919) whose 1918 work, *Serair al-Kur'an* (Secrets of the Quran) "maintained that the verses on cosmic events (later called 'cosmic verses') in the Holy Quran, which is revealed by God, should be congruent with the truth attained by modern science," according to Muslim scholar Ekmeleddin Ihsanoglu.[33] In a mode similar to Galileo, Pasha maintained that if scientific truth is in conflict with Quranic verses, "then the latter need be interpreted."

This has continued into late twentieth century of finding in the pages of Muslim Holy Book a "miraculous scientific nature."[34] Examples are presented from a book 1400 years old presenting scientific insights before its time, such as the moon's light being derivative from the sun (Quran 10:5), and the Big Bang in the phrase "the heavens and the earth were sewn together and We rent them asunder" (Quran 21:30), and the essence of the scientific method with its call to "produce proof" to discern truth (Quran 2:111).[35]

This movement is wildly popular in Islam today. As Guessoum says, "It's by far the most popular cultural trend in the Arab and Muslim world today,"[36] and it has its proponents in the United States as well. Islam is not alone. This type of scriptural interpretation occurs in Hinduism and Christianity, even in the assertions that Buddhist texts teach a "science of the mind." But is it legitimate? Iqbal concludes about this movement of scientific tafsir, "Attempts to interpret the Quran scientifically, therefore, suffer from the inherent disparity between Quranic and modern scientific views of the cosmos."[37]

But there may be more at play. I return to my conversation with Telliel about rhetoric:[38] Scientific *tafsir* seeks

> its own field and the connections with modern science in attempting to be rational and evidentialist. There is both a kind of scholarly dimension, and there is also a defensive dimension. You can also add that there is certain kind of literalism in seeking to combine science and Islam and particular way of thinking about Scripture.

My ears perked up when he commented, "It's a genre that's easy to reproduce—and thus a 'portable discourse.'" It does not require you to engage with tradition of *tafsir*, and perhaps that's why it can be so popular. "Of course, this happens in Hinduism (the Vedas have knowledge of airplanes[39]), as well as Christianity." In many ways, this is not truly scientific, but a religious discourse. The Quran then becomes a "site or source of enchantment," which makes sense because of divine signs, and this revitalizes their commitment.

In some ways, Telliel continued: this highlights a way of thinking about cosmos (and I'll add, one that coheres with Nasr's perspective). It reflects the problem with "modern science and its way of reading the universe. Instead, scientific *tafsir* presents a 'positive' approach to science." Let it be said that it's an approach forged in the fires of missionary attacks from Christians who often asserted that Muslims cannot build a scientific society. Indeed, it is part of how "Muslim intellectuals have responded: Islam is pro-science."

Islam and evolution

At times, this commitment to the Quran, and its narratives of God's creation, is expressed with a resistance to Darwinian thought (which is not quite the same as contemporary evolutionary science), an extreme example of which is the Turkish creationist Adnan Oktar under the pen name Harun Yahya. Though discredited on many accounts and in prison, Oktar's *The Evolution Deceit: The Scientific Collapse of Darwinism and Its Ideological Background* from the year 2000[40] is still influential. Many scholars note that what is happening in Islamic creationism is similar to the promotion of anti-evolution throughout the world, and that it draws from not only young earth creationism but also the Intelligent Design movement.

Naturally, not all Muslims follow Oktar, nor are they anti-evolution. Though some studies indicate that about half of American Muslims accept evolution (split evenly between "due to natural processes" and "God's design"),[41] Guessoum estimates that "no more than 15 percent of Muslim respondents accept evolution."[42] "A Pew Research Center survey of Muslims worldwide conducted in 2011 and 2012 found that a 22-public median of 53% said they believed humans and other living things evolved over time."[43] Guessoum, on the other hand, cites research to indicate that "about 60% rejecting it outright."[44] This diversity of opinion may be behind his statement: "Indeed, there is no uniform Islamic position on the theory of evolution."[45]

The key sticking point is the creation of Adam. The clearest reading of the Quran is that God created Adam directly, though God used material from the earth. "We created man from sounding clay, from mud molded into shape" (quoted previously). And "He began the creation of man from clay, and made his progeny from a quintessence of fluid" (32:7–8). For example, scholar of Islamic theology and legal theory David Solomon Jalajel has concluded, "The following is apparent textual evidence: Adam was created directly by God directly from earth. Both Adam and his wife were created by God without the agency of parents," adding "These are the conclusions that have been reached by all orthodox commentators."[46] This does seem to be the majority report, as it were.

At the same time, it's worth noting that some commentators "consider Adam a representative of humanity rather than a specific individual."[47] Quran interpreter Ghulam Ahmad Parvez writes,

> What the Quran has stated in different verses indicates that the person expelled from *jannah* [the Garden] was not any specific man, but a metaphorical representative of humanity. In other words, the story of Adam is not the story of one particular person (or couple), but the Tale of Man which the Quran has told metaphorically.[48]

In addition, the creative (and somewhat controversial) scholar Muhammad Shahrour has noted a distinction in the Quran's use of two terms— *insan* ("man" or "human being") and *bashar* (though often translated "human being," it is only used in creation of the species before it evolved to *insan*). Guessoum summarizes this perspective, "In other words, *bashar* is identified with the hominid stage of human evolution or even earlier species [of the genus] Homo, and *insan* with 'modern man.'"[49]

Technology and transhumanism

One common conception of Islam is of a religion entirely resistant to the influences of modernity.

I asked Guessoum about transhumanism, and he underscored that Muslim thinkers are definitely engaging in this topic,[50] "realizing that it is not in the realm of science fiction." In fact, "many biohackers have modified their bodies by inserting chips that can control or be controlled at a distance," such as Elon Musk's Neuralink Company. I thought his ethical comments were particularly important, highlighting the distinction, which Muslim scholars make, between unnecessary enhancements and corrective procedures (like prosthetics), citing Quran 4:119 that warns against modifying humans, animals, and rest of creation. The verse quotes Satan and God's reply, " 'I will certainly mislead them and delude them with empty hopes. Also, I will order them and they will slit the ears of cattle and alter Allah's creation.' And whoever takes Satan as a guardian instead of Allah has certainly suffered a tremendous loss."

In view of space, let me close with one, perhaps slightly extreme, example. Tracy Trothern and Calvin Mercer in their textbook on transhumanism, AI, biohacking and religion comment on Roy Jackson's *Muslim and Supermuslim: The Quest for the Perfect Being and Beyond*, "a recent book about Islam and transhumanism illustrates how a 'creative and explorative' approach to the religion positions Islam as an inspirational and productive interlocutor in the debate about radical human enhancement."[51] I add this because to many ears, Islam sounds like it is fixated on past revelation and lacks lack openness to new science and technology. In fact, that is not the case.

Science, ethics, and Islam

Contemporary Muslims live in societies deeply affected by science. Telliel reminded me that

> these conversations about science and faith happen through organ donation, secular law, IVF, what governments and society think about their society. It's not as much as whether Islam is compatible with modern science generally, it's also how to think about debt and elderly, nuclear weapons.

And so, what "Islam and science" means is not about people outside of space and time in some very defined and narrow interaction with contemporary discoveries. Telliel brought me back to the importance of "ethical reasoning" in addressing science and technology.

Ethical reasoning meets us regularly, across the country (and the globe) with climate change. The Islamic response has been clear. Consider the November 2016 Statement of Dr. Azhar Azeez President of the Islamic Society of North America, the largest US Muslim umbrella organization,

> According to Islam's most basic and fundamental teachings, human beings have been uniquely charged with the great responsibility of being Guardians and Caretakers of the Earth. It goes against the overall service based mission ISNA, to invest in fossil fuel companies whose operations and products cause such grave harm to humanity and to Creation and ISNA commits herself to this cause.[52]

And this on the website *Interfaith and Climate Change*:

> There is now a growing awareness of the damage that has been wrought upon our earthly home through human-induced climate

change, loss of biodiversity and pollution. This is substantiated by a scientific consensus that we are threatening our own survival through our abuse of the natural world. We need to act now if we are to ensure that we are leaving behind a liveable Earth for future generations and seek guidance from the Quran and Sunnah to show us the way: Corruption has appeared in the land and the sea by what the hands of humankind have wrought, that He may let them taste some consequences of their deeds, so that they may turn back.[53]

(Quran 30:41)

Naturally, what this means for the average Muslim is variable. But clearly there is no reason to resist efforts to combat climate change and excellent Quranic reasons for doing so. Guessoum concludes that "this in fact is a duty for Muslims."[54]

Final thoughts

Though it's complicated to summarize a religion this vast and diverse, we can definitely say that Islam has a glorious history with science. A variety of voices also assess that Islam has an uneven relationship with modern science today, not least because the word "science" too often brings with it the connotation "Euro-American." Dallal has shared his assessment that can serve as a summary statement,

> The main problem is that the Arabo-Islamic scientific culture is a legacy of the past and a hope for the future but absent, in effect, in the present. Much of the debate about science in the modern period focuses on bridging the gap between the lost past and the desired future.[55]

For my part, I'll add that the Islamic world, and its one-fifth of the world's population, stands at an inflection point with science and that it possesses a treasure trove of resources for a productive future.

Suggestions for further reading

There are some truly excellent sources if you'd like to go further in understanding Islam and science. For a straightforward, easy-to-access introduction, I'd head to Nidhal Guessom, *The Young Muslim's Guide to Modern Science* (Manchester: Beacon Books, 2018). More intricating and worth the effort is the collected essays edited by Ted Peters, Muzaffar Iqbal, and Syed Nomanul Haq, *God, Life, and the Cosmos: Christian and*

Islamic Perspectives (Aldershot: Ashgate, 2002). To go further, see Ahmad Dallal, *Islam, Science, and the Challenge of History* (New Haven, CT: Yale University Press, 2010); Muzzaffar Iqbal, *Islam and Science* (Aldershot: Ashgate, 2002); and though written decades ago, still good, Seyyed Hossein Nasr, *Science and Civilization in Islam* (Cambridge, MA: Harvard University Press, 1968).

Notes

1 Ahmad Dallal, *Islam, Science, and the Challenge of History* (New Haven, CT: Yale University Press, 2010), 1.
2 Pew Research Center, "Chapter 7: Religion, Science and Popular Culture," 30 April 2013, www.pewforum.org/2013/04/30/the-worlds-muslims-religion-politics-society-science-and-popular-culture, accessed 15 June 2022.
3 Edward Said, "Impossible Histories: Why the Many Islams Cannot Be Simplified," *Harper's Magazine*, July 2002, 69–74.
4 Prothero, *God Is Not One*, 28.
5 John L. Esposito, ed., *The Oxford Dictionary of Islam* (Oxford: Oxford University Press, 2003), 317.
6 Daniel Brown, *A New Introduction to* Islam, 3rd ed. (Oxford: Wiley Blackwell, 2017), 266.
7 Dallal, 154.
8 See Seyyed Hossein Nasr, "Islam and Science," in *The Oxford Handbook of Religion and Science*, ed. Philip Clayton, assoc. ed. Zachary Simpson (Oxford: Oxford University Press, 2006), 78ff.
9 Steve Paulson, *Atoms and Eden: Conversations on Religion and Science* (Oxford: Oxford University Press, 2010), 222.
10 Guessom, www.youtube.com/watch?v=lG0pFgm8APw. See also his interview with Steve Paulson, *Atoms and Eden*, 215ff.
11 In Steve Paulson, *Atoms and Eden: Conversations on Religion and Science* (Oxford: Oxford University Press, 2010).
12 Ibid., 220, 219.
13 Nidhal Guessom, "Islam and Science," February 2022, https://video.ibm.com/recorded/131412015, accessed 15 June 2022.
14 Guessoum, *Young Muslim's Guide*, 19.
15 Al-Ghazali, *Moderation in Belief*, trans. Michael Marmura, "Al-Ghazali's Chapter on Divine Power in the Iqtisad," *Arabic Sciences and Philosophy* 4 (1994): 279–315.
16 *Oxford Dictionary of Islam*, 239.
17 Alister McGrath, *Science and Religion: A New* Introduction, 2nd ed. (Oxford: Wiley-Blackwell, 2010), 138.
18 Huston Smith, *The World's Religions* (New York: Harper SanFrancisco, 1991), 227.
19 Muzaffir Iqbal, "Scientific Commentary on the Quran," in *The Study Quran: A New Translation and Commentary*, ed. Seyyed Hossein Nazr (New York: HarperOne, 2015), 1693.
20 Ekmeleddin Ihsanoglu, "Modern Islam," in *Science and Religion Around the World*, eds. John Hedley Brooke and Ronald L. Numbers (Oxford: Oxford University Press, 2011), 170.

21 Nasr, "Islam and Science," 75.
22 Ibid., 76.
23 Ibid., 85.
24 Guessom, *Young Muslim's Guide*, 101.
25 Ibid., 109.
26 Unless otherwise noted, the rendering of these Quranic verses is found here: www.clearquran.com/015.html, accessed 14 June 2022.
27 Cited by William Lane Craig, *Reasonable Faith* (Chicago, IL: Moody Press, 1994), 80.
28 Cited by Golshani, "Creation in the Islamic Outlook and in Modern Cosmology," in *God, Life, and the Cosmos*, eds. Ted Peters, Muzaffar Iqbal, and Syed Nomanul Haq (London: Routledge Press, 2021), 225.
29 Cf. Dallal, 169.
30 Iqbal, *The Study Quran,* 1682.
31 Guessoum, *Young Muslim's Guide*, 101–2.
32 Ibid., 106.
33 Ihsanoglu, "Modern Islam," 168.
34 Ibid., 169.
35 As one example, in a reasonably popular TEDx talk, Omar Abdul Fatah presents, "Using Logic and Science to Establish Faith: An Islamic Perspective," 31 March 2018, www.youtube.com/watch?v=0L8KjLtcNQE, accessed 15 June 2022.
36 Guessoum in Paulson, *Atoms and Eden*, 225.
37 Iqbal, *The Study Quran*, 1693.
38 See also Yunus Doğan Telliel, "Miraculous Evidence: Scientific Wonders and Religious Reasons," *Comparative Studies of South Asia, Africa and the Middle East* 39.3 (2019): 528–42; and "Introduction: Studying Evidence and Religion in Post-Truth Times," *Comparative Studies of South Asia, Africa and the Middle East* 39.3 (2019): 495–9.
39 See Rami Lakshmi, "Indians Invented Planes 7,000 Years Ago—and Other Startling Claims at the Science Congress," 4 January 2015, *Washington Post*, www.washingtonpost.com/news/worldviews/wp/2015/01/04/indians-invented-planes-7000-years-ago-and-other-startling-claims-at-the-science-congress, accessed 14 June 2022.
40 London: Ta-Ha Publishers, Ltd.
41 *Pew Research Center*, "Views about Human Evolution," www.pewresearch.org/religion/religious-landscape-study/views-about-human-evolution, accessed 15 June 2022.
42 Guessoum, *Atoms and Eden*, 225.
43 Pew, "On the Intersection of Science and Religion," 9 February 2021, *Trend Magazine*, www.pewtrusts.org/en/trend/archive/winter-2021/on-the-intersection-of-science-and-religion, accessed 15 June 2022.
44 Guessom, *Young Muslim's Guide*, 113.
45 Ibid.
46 David Solomon Jalajel, "Tawaqquf and the Acceptance of Human Evolution," https://f.hubspotusercontent10.net/hubfs/4713562/Website-Paper-PDFs/Tawaqquf%20and%20Acceptance%20of%20Human%20Evolution%20-%20David%20Jalajel%20(1).pdf, accessed 15 June 2022.
47 Iqbal, *The Study Quran*, 1687.
48 Ghulan Ahmad Parvez, *Lughat al-Quran* (Lahore: Adarah Talu-e Islam, 1960), 1:214; cited in Muzaffir Iqbal, *The Study Quran*, 1687.

49 Guessom, *Young Muslim's Guide*, 117, citing Muhammad Shahrour, *Al-Kitab wal Quran: qura'a mu' asirah* (The Book and the Koran: a modern reading), Damascus, 1990.

50 Private email from Nidhal Guessoum 14 June 2022. See also, H. Mavani, "God's Deputy: Islam and Transhumanism," in *Transhumanism and the Body. The World Religions Speak*, eds. C. Mercer and D. F. Maher (New York: Palgrave Macmillan, 2014), 67–84; A. I. Bouzenita, "'The Most Dangerous Idea?' Islamic Deliberations on Transhumanism," *Darulfunun Ilahiyat* 29, no. 2 (2018): 201–28; S. Hejazi, "'Humankind. The Best of Molds'—Islam Confronting Transhumanism," *Sophia* 58 (2019): 677–88.

51 Calvin Mercer and Tracy J. Trothen, *Religion and the Technological Future an Introduction to Biohacking, Artificial Intelligence, and Transhumanism* (London: Macmillan Palgrave, 2002), 36.

52 "Islamic Society of North America Announces Divest-Invest Commitment," 10 November 2016, https://fore.yale.edu/files/Islamic_Society.pdf, accessed 15 June 2022.

53 "Interfaith and Climate: Multifaith Responses to Climate Change," https://www.cop26interfaith.com/?p=546, accessed 19 September 2022.

54 Guessoum, *Young Muslim's Guide*, 136.

55 Dallal, 150.

8 Connections both old and new

Hinduism and science

As we begin a look at Hinduism and science, let's consider a popular *Times of India* article by journalist Dipanakar Gupta:

> As Hinduism is an idol-centric religion, its core principles are of no consequence to science. Christianity is a creation-centric religion. This is why it had to oppose modern science which, too, is creation-centric. The latter has taken strong positions on how life began, how day became night, and how our beings are energised. This is what compelled science and religion to go on a collision course in the western world. From the 16th century onwards, they were like two monster trucks driving in opposite directions on a one-way street. Hinduism was spared all this.[1]

There's more to say about Hindu cosmology—which I will do later—but this article seems to demonstrate that it's difficult not to compare any particular religion's interaction with science with Christianity's. And aside from some traces of Hindu triumphalism, Guptka's provocative introduction underscores that Hinduism's approach to science is something completely different for many, especially if we come to science and religion solely defined (either for good or ill) as science and Christianity.

In other words, Hinduism is a clear case that a relationship with science can look very different from our expectations. And as I've mentioned, one of the primary reasons I've written this book is to address science from the perspective of a particular religion, not as "non-Christian religions" or "other religions." Elaine Howard Ecklund recounts meeting Ravi, who grew up in India, where he received most of his training and science, and who now works in a US science lab. She asked Ravi how he thought scientists should respond to religious resistance to evolution in public schools. After reflecting, he responded, "Why do you Americans talk so much about conflict between religion and science? We Hindus

DOI: 10.4324/9781003214236-8

never talk in such terms. Our religion only makes us think more deeply about the ways that science allows us to see the world of the gods."[2]

Indeed, Hinduism and science are generally seen to be well-suited. Let's take in what the Pew Research Center has found: "The predominant view among Hindus who were interviewed is that science and Hinduism are related and compatible." And on the particularly contentious topic for some religions, evolution, Pew found that "80% of Hindus in the U.S. said humans and other living things have evolved over time, with majorities also saying this was due to natural processes."[3]

Though the origins of Hinduism are a bit complex, it is perhaps the oldest religion in this book. And, its roots go deep in India. For that reason, though this book focuses on the United States, I cannot overlook the importance of the historical interaction between science and Hinduism in India. And though Hinduism has made deep and ancient contributions to science, it is underappreciated contemporarily, at least in the United States. Therefore, some of its contributions might sound fresh. Finally, as a classic example of an Eastern religion, Hinduism provides a fresh perspective for those familiar with western approaches and thus an excellent contrast in many ways with monotheism.

Introducing Hinduism: one last lightning round Q & A

In just a few questions and answers, I attempt to outline the contours of the broad tradition of Hinduism.

What are its origins and history?

This is an Indigenous religion of India as developed to present day, with the oral tradition it is grounded in dating back to as early as 2200 BCE. Even the word *Hindu* is based on the Indus River valley. The words *Hindu* and *India* are related by common linguistic roots, and Hinduism is firmly rooted in the soil of India, where about 80% of its 1.4 billion people are Hindu,[4] and where approximately 90% of the world's Hindus live. There are approximately about 1.2 billion, or about 15% of the world's population, which makes it the third largest religion in the world.

How many Hindus are in the United States?

In the United States, Hindus are about 0.7% of the population.[5] According to Harvard Divinity School, most of the 2.5 million Hindus in the United States are immigrants,[6] with New York, Chicago, and San

Francisco as the top three destinations.[7] Notably, Indian Americans are more likely than Americans generally to work in scientific and technological fields.[8]

What about gods and the universe?

What we call Hinduism today is stunningly diverse. In Hinduism, there is one Supreme Reality (Brahman) manifested in many gods and goddesses. Many Hindus—and scholars of Hinduism—simply use "God" and "Brahman" interchangeably. Others note how Brahman is distinguished from the western monotheistic personal God: According to French scholar of metaphysics Rene Guenon, Brahman is "'beyond all distinctions (*nirvishesha*)' and 'beyond all qualities (*nirguna*).'"[9]

Out of the millions of actual gods and goddesses, a few stand out. The elephant god, Ganesh, is a favorite, and the three principal deities of Hinduism, Vishnu, the preserver, Shiva, the destroyer, and Mahadevi/ Shakti, "great goddess" (the latter replacing Brahma, the creator).

What about other religions then?

Hindus often emphasize common themes with other religions as well. After quoting Depok Chopra's "You and I are the same beings," leading scholar of science and religion Philip Clayton writes, "This Hindu emphasis tends to lift attention above the specific doctrinal (historical, philosophical) claims defended by the different religions and to concentrate attention instead on what they share in common."[10]

Is there a founder like the Buddha or Muhammed?

Simply put: No. And that's one characteristic (at least) that makes Hinduism a fascinating religious tradition. Naturally, some key figures have emerged like Ramakrishna and Swami Vivekananda in the nineteenth century, as well as Mahatma Gandhi in the twentieth century, as well as some of the contemporary figures you'll meet in this chapter.

One last time with Prothero's problem–solution structure: What are the human situation and life's purpose?

Humans are in bondage to ignorance and illusion but have the ability to escape. Rebirth through the wheel of samsara is based on one's action and the karma they produce. The purpose is to gain release from rebirth (reincarnation or transmigration of souls), or at least a better rebirth.

So, let's be clear: is there an afterlife?

Reincarnation continues until we gain enlightenment, and thus the release from samsara. After enlightenment, the soul (the *atman*) rejoins the Supreme Reality (Brahman).

What are key Hindu practices?

Hindus practice their religious life through meditation, worship (*puja*) and devotion to a god or goddess, various forms of yoga (meaning "yoking" oneself to a life path) pilgrimage to holy cities, and overall living according to one's dharma (that is one's role or purpose).

What about central texts?

The key texts you'll see referenced here are the Vedas, Upanishads, and Bhagavad Gita. Composition dates attributed to the *Rig Veda*, the oldest of the Vedas, are 1700–1500 BCE. The Upanishads are more difficult to date because of their varying content and authorship, but scholars set a range from the seventh century BCE to the first century CE.

Are those texts differentiated in any way?

There are two designations. There are *smriti*, literally "that which is remembered," a group of texts customarily ascribed to an author, and these have traditionally been written down. They are differentiated from the authorless *srutis*, which were passed on verbally throughout generations and have become fixed.

Two scholars for this chapter: Victoria Price and Vijaya Nagarajan

To understand Hinduism's relationship with science, I talked with Berkeley's Graduate Theological Union and Center for Dharma Studies scholar Victoria Price. Her expertise is the intersection of religion and technology, and specifically how American Hindu groups use the internet to connect with practitioners. Or as she commented, "I'm fascinated by the way people communicate online and how religious people and institutions function in online spaces."[11] She is a lively conversant both in realtime and via email, and she opened new vistas on contemporary Hinduism in the United States. In addition, I had conversations with Vijaya Nagarajan, associate professor in the Department of Theology and Religious Studies and in the Program of Environmental Studies.

In light of Price's contributions, and because technology is central to the lives of many American Hindus, I'll move to technology after a brief foray into the history of Hinduism and science and a few general comments.

History of Hinduism, history of science

As with Islam previously, I need to reach back in time for a secure grasp of Hinduism. In addition, its history with science in the United States is inextricably linked with its history in India for at least two reasons: most Hindus live in India, and most American Hindus are immigrants or children of immigrants.

There were some early inroads of Hindu philosophy and scripture into the United States. A striking example is Henry David Thoreau's reflections in his famous 1854 *Walden* (and I am keeping his original spelling),

> In the morning I bathe my intellect in the stupendous and cosmogonal philosophy of the Bhagvat Geeta, since whose composition years of the gods have elapsed, and in comparison with which our modern world and its literature seem puny and trivial; and I doubt if that philosophy is not to be referred to a previous state of existence, so remote is its sublimity from our conceptions. I lay down the book and go to my well for water, and lo! there I meet the servant of the Bramin, priest of Brahma and Vishnu and Indra, who still sits in his temple on the Ganges reading the Vedas, or dwells at the root of a tree with his crust and water jug. I meet his servant come to draw water for his master, and our buckets as it were grate together in the same well. The pure Walden water is mingled with the sacred water of the Ganges.[12]

Thoreau brought Hindu thought to Walden—and thus to many who had not encountered Vishnu or the Bhagavad Gita—and he's drawing on ideas almost 4,000 years old. This long expanse of history allows me to insert the scientific advances of Hindu culture in various places.

Hinduism has made deep and ancient contributions to science. As "the father of chemical science in India" Bengali scientist P.C. Ray has written, "India was the cradle of mathematical and chemical sciences."[13] Let me offer one example in the history of Hindu science. One key advance occurred in the fourth century CE when Indian mathematicians developed a decimal-value numeration, with nine digits and a zero, which was subsequently misnamed "Arabic numerals" after their adoption by Islamic mathematicians.[14] It's hard to overstate the importance of this breakthrough for the mathematical skills needed to advance science and, more recently, for its direct effect on the 0s and 1s of the digital world.

And yet, because of colonialism, the encounter of Hinduism in India with modern science represents a complicated history. As Jawaharlal Nehru University Professor Makarand Paranjape writes, "Under colonialism, traditional Indian spirituality encountered modern Western ideas, including modern science."[15] The theme of a critical engagement with modern science—because of its inextricable European connections—returns and will recur throughout this chapter.

Paranjape then offers this synopsis,

> If we revert to Ian Barbour's classic formulation of a fourfold typology of conflict, independence, dialogue and integration, we notice that in India all four types of relationships have been present both in the past and in the present, but that conflict has never been predominant, unlike in the West. Moreover, while a number of practising scientists stress the independence of the two domains, a number of spiritual leaders have advocated both dialogue and integration.[16]

German-Canadian scholar of Hinduism and Indian culture and history, Klaus Klostermaier presents a more unified view when he writes,

> Hinduism never knew the Western antagonism between philosophy and theology, nor does it have a history of warfare between science and religion. It was the highest aim of Hindus to find *satyam*, truth/reality, which could be approached in many ways and appear in many forms.[17]

Like all the religions we are considering, the encounter of Hinduism with science is hard to summarize.

Nagarajan told me that there doesn't seem to be a natural antipathy to science; there's no anti-Darwinianism, no resistance to vaccine. "There's no conflict as far as I can tell." (Her father in fact was one of the founders of large Hindu temples in the United States and primarily worked with scientists and technologists.) Partly, as we will see, there is no fixed interpretation of hermeneutic of sacred texts. Hindus look at texts from a "multi-centeredness," which, Nagarajan affirmed, brings deep humility alongside literal truth. In that way, it's like a guiding scientific hermeneutic, which doesn't stay with a fixed interpretation of reality, but adapts new information and testing until it finds truth.

So far, these general comments are promising, though one suspects the reality is a bit less neat than this summary. Let's look at biological evolution briefly.

The specific case of evolution

In surveying responses to biological evolution, scholar of Hinduism and science C. Mackenzie Brown has noted a variety of responses to

Darwinism "from outright rejection to fairly robust but limited accommodation."[18] In fact, this is similar to what the Pew Research Center discovered (in this case, in a global survey):

> Evolution posed no conflict for the Hindus interviewed, who said the concept of evolution was encompassed in their religious teachings. "In Hinduism we have something like this as well, that tells us we originated from different species, which is why we also believe in reincarnation, and how certain deities take different forms. This is why certain animals are seen as sacred animals, because it's one of the forms that this particular deity had taken," said a 29-year-old Hindu woman in Singapore.[19]

This means that Hindus didn't run into a preconception of the fixity of species like the west did, a tradition which ran all the way from Aristotle through the Victorian scientists in England.

At the same time, Darwin himself didn't have much room for God in his theory of biological evolution, and so Hindu thinkers don't ingest Darwin's thought and its materialism whole. Hindu social reformer and philosopher Keshab Chandra Sen described evolution as "the great idea of the day" in 1877, and continued, "The question perhaps is not so serious after all, whether men descended from lower animals. But whether there is a progressive evolution going on in the individual life of man is a question in which we are all interested."[20]

Technology and Hinduism

India is a leader in the high-tech industry, and similarly, many American Hindus are in high-tech fields in the United States. This connection has led to an emerging field of "Digital Hinduism."[21] Hinduism and technology were my particular interest in my conversation with Price.

Overall, technology has afforded Hinduism a wider audience. And so, I asked Price (and I paraphrase our conversation), "How does technology affect Hinduism?" Generally, she answered, technology is creating a wider virtual audience. In addition, since a large percentage of Hindus in this country are immigrants, there is an abiding interest in connecting with religious life in India. The internet and social media have given Hindus in the United States a remarkable access to ashrams and meditation centers in India. Specifically, virtual connections allow Hindus to offer online worship, or *puja*, where another proxy worshipper offers elements for ritual at a Hindu temple. And since "some Hindus who are of the belief that because Brahman (or God) exists within everything," Price told me,

"Brahman is also in the technology that humans have created. From that view, there's no negative feeling toward using technology during or as a part of worship because the essence of Brahman exists within it."

But afterward, I wondered, and I emailed Price with the question, *Are there problems between Hinduism and technology?* Her reply started with our previous conversation,

> I don't think I emphasized the importance of embodiment enough. So many Hindu rituals rely on the physical acts of chanting mantras aloud, waving the sacred flame or the incense in front of the murti (statue representing the deity), circumambulating the altar, etc. These acts are difficult to replicate if the practitioner is engaging in the kind of "puja by proxy" that I spoke about or if they are viewing a livestream of a ritual on their device. There is also an issue of purity that comes into play when using electronic devices for worship. If, for example, a devotee downloads a picture of a deity to their phone and sets their phone on their home altar to use the picture for puja, they may feel the need to ritually cleanse their phone before placing it on the altar in the same way they would cleanse an offering of fruit that they would offer during worship.

There indeed is a particular way of relating to the non-human, even mechanical, in science and this brought to mind an experience from Ecklund's 2012–15 RASIC research initiative[22] (Religion Among Scientists in International Context), which involved an multi-country study aimed at understanding how scientists view the social context of science. There, at the public gathering at Rice University when the findings were reported, one story struck me: Hindu scientists offered *puja* to their technical scientific instruments.

This connection with technology has in fact been picked up by Hindu religious leaders, or *sadhus*, who, as Antoinette Elizabeth DeNapoli, writes,

> emphasize by means of storytelling three narrative motifs that articulate the divinity of technology. These are: Sannyās represents the "original technology" and the "original science"; technology manifests the properties of creativity and change that characterize what the sadhus associate with "the nature of Brahman" and "the rule of dharm"; and, finally, the apocalyptic Kalki avatār concept offers a redemptive metaphor for the evolving human-technology interface in the current global milieu.[23]

And so, the technological flow is not just from the worshipper to virtual *puja* but also moves from religious leader to follower.

In fact, virtual spaces have allowed for the emergence of "Mediatized gurus" like Hanna Mannila and Xenia Zeiler, that is, leaders within the Hindu traditions that present themselves online, often through Facebook.[24] This allows for a curated and potentially universal presence. Let it be said that the digital media certainly affects the message and the perception of the messenger. Previously, gurus taught through classrooms.

> But a website is public and open to view for anyone with access to the Internet, at any time. Therefore, gurus seem to have to create an image and brand of themselves—willingly or not, knowingly or not—and authority construction plays an important role in this.[25]

Once again, technology is both a vehicle for religion—and in this case, Hinduism—and shapes it in the process.

Concerning cosmology

One key flashpoint for religion and science is when a religious tradition and its texts have a very specific teaching of how the world came to be, or a fixed doctrine of creation.

A notion of the world's creation tied to a sacred text can also imply a relatively young earth—in fact Christian young-earth creationists talk about a 6,000- to 10,000-year-old creation. Huston Smith describes the diametrically opposed view of Hinduism via story:

> The Himalayas, is said, are made of solid granite. Once every thousand years a bird flies over them with a silk scarf in its beak, brushing their peaks with a scarf. When by this process the Himalayas have been worn away, one day of a cosmic cycle will have elapsed.[26]

The famous scientist Carl Sagan added this about Hinduism:

> It is the only religion in which the time scales correspond to modern scientific cosmology . . . 8.64 billion years long. Longer than the age of the Earth or the Sun and about half the time since the Big Bang.[27]

Similarly, historians of science Tomoko Yoshida and Stephen P. Weldon conclude, "one can find proponents of Hindu cosmology who argue for much, much longer periods of time than the current scientific status accepts."[28]

All this is certainly fascinating. As honorary professor at the National Institute of Advanced Studies in Bangalore B.V. Subbarayappa has written, "Hindus generally accept God as Creator, and some embrace a personal God, most believe that the Creator is immanent in the created world."[29] And yet, what creation means differs markedly from what western monotheism presents.

In summarizing contemporary Hindu views of cosmology, Canadian scholar of bioethics and religious studies Harold Coward writes this in the *Encyclopedia of Science and Religion*, drawing on insights from Hindu seers or *rishis*. He is so clear and comprehensive that I will cite his length:

> Hindu thinkers approach the still unresolved mystery of the universe by looking back to Brahman (the Divine) as somehow associated with the creation or production of the universe. Scientific theory has speculated that the universe may arise from a quantum vacuum state, which is a peculiar mixture of emptiness and activity . . . . The universe is ontologically characterized by the term *Brahman* from the root *brh* "to expand." The *rishis* thought of the universe as an "expanding Brahman," which is consistent with contemporary cosmological thinking. The current idea of a Big Bang in which very dense matter explodes into an expanding universe is seen to be prefigured by the Upanishadic notion *bindu*—a dimensionless point that is a unity of both static and dynamic forces, the dynamic expressing itself as the universe of multiplicity while essentially remaining a unity or order (*rta*). Or, as cosmologists put it, about 100 billion stars, including the sun, make up the Milky Way galaxy, a spiral wheel-shaped structure. This galaxy is part of a group of galaxies that form a cluster, while clusters in turn form superclusters of many thousands of galaxies. Cosmologists suggest that this pattern of hierarchical clustering prevails throughout the cosmos with gravitational forces holding the whole thing together.[30]

Coward points to the Upanishads, and specifically the words of the Yajnavalkya to his pupil Aruni: "This world and the next world and all beings and all natural phenomena are strung together by the thread, the Inner Controller, the Immortal, the Brahman" (*Brhadarañyaka Upanishad* III:7:3).

Let me offer additional nuance to these insights because, in Hindu sacred texts, one finds various cosmological statements as well as a plethora of interpretations. Sangeetha Menon, Fellow at the National Institute of Advanced Studies in Bangalore comments, on the

> non-existence of anything prior to creation—we find Upanishadic references like "There was nothing whatsoever here in the beginning"

(*Brhadaranyaka Upanishad*, I.2.1); "Non-existence verily was this (world) in the beginning" (*Taittiriya Upanishad* II.7.1); "In the beginning this (world) was non-existent" (*Chandogya Upanishad* III.19.1). From another angle of explaining creation, *Aitareya Upanishad* speaks of the creator's entrance into the body by opening in the skull—*vidriti*,[31]

which obviously indicates something pre-existent and thus a cyclical universe. This points to what Coward adds: the expansive array of Hindu scripture allows "ample room for speculations."[32]

In fact, the *Rigveda* contains the Nasadiya sukta hymn which does not offer a cosmological theory but asks cosmological questions about the nature of universe and how it began:

Darkness there was at first, by darkness hidden;
Without distinctive marks, this all was water;
That which, becoming, by the void was covered;
That One by force of heat came into being;
Who really knows? Who will here proclaim it?
Whence was it produced? Whence is this creation?
Gods came afterwards, with the creation of this universe.
Who then knows whence it has arisen?
Whether God's will created it, or whether He was mute;
Perhaps it formed itself, or perhaps it did not;
Only He who is its overseer in highest heaven knows,
Only He knows, or perhaps He does not know.

Rigveda 10:129

Flexible interpretations

One way to put this is that multiple stories of creation exist in Hinduism. As Menon writes about the *rishi* in the Upanishads, "The Upanishadic Rishi considers any doctrine of creation or causality as a myth created to explain mystery."[33] Put another way, fundamentalist or strict literalist approaches to sacred texts usually raise problems with experimental science, as we have seen in Islam and Christianity. In Hinduism, although some fundamentalism exists, it is rarely about the sacred texts. As scholar of Hinduism Daniel Gold comments, "The idea of Vedic authority known to traditional Hindus is much more diffuse and abstract than the idea of a closed biblical canon known to the West."[34]

I've mentioned that if we are to call the Hindu cosmologies "creation," then are creation in their own way. In a classic phrase from Hinduism, atman (our self or soul) is Brahman (the Divine or God). This is the classic view of pantheism (God is everywhere throughout the universe and thus all is divine) or monism (all is one). And thus, there is a unity in all study: mystical is scientific and vice versa. And this idea often is called divine imminence—where God is close. In the following paragraphs, I'll note the effect on care for the environment.

With these positive reflections in mind, it's worth taking a step back to ponder whether a flexible doctrine of scripture prevents or allows for a true collaboration, a real give-and-take with science. Is the relationship between science and any particular religious text better when the latter both demands little and offers a striking variability of options for interpretation? Flexibility affords no ultimate conflicts.

Focus on consciousness

At the heart of Hindu cosmology is mind or consciousness. In fact, the world is dependent on consciousness. Menon summarizes what the Upanishads teach: "(i) space-time-event creation is an illusory projection of the transcendental Truth, and (ii) the experience of the world as 'other' is the result of self-ignorance."[35]

This means, of course, that Hinduism is committed to the existence of the non-material *atman* and studying consciousness, which cannot be entirely reduced to material processes of the brain. It also worth taking a step back and noticing that the existence of a non-material soul is not amenable to the testing of modern science. As Clayton writes, "This focus on an eternal soul has led to some conflict with Western scientists and their approaches to the study of the human person."[36]

Some interpretations of quantum physics make mind central to physical reality—the indeterminacy of the wave function needs perception to become some real—and this also connects with Hindu thought. Menon certainly leans on this when she criticizes a translation of the Hindu concept of *maya* as "illusion,"

> The growing interest in the ideas of quantum entanglement and multiple possible worlds by quantum physicists might provide a welcome note for the dynamic and positive interpretations of maya, which hold that the world is "real while experiencing, but not independently."[37]

In other words, as we've seen with other religions, quantum physics is brought in to provide support for the interrelation of consciousness and the material world. Though very much in keeping with physicists David Bohm and Fritjof Capra, I need to underline that this is not the view of quantum physics in the predominant model of the Copenhagen Interpretation.

A note on ayurveda

Alongside modern science in India, there has always been traditional science as well, such as *ayurveda*. Paranjape writes, "Ayurveda, as its name suggests, was described as the fifth Veda, thus not only linked to the Vedas but sharing its worldview and notions of wellness, modern, Western medicine was seen as wholly secular, if more effective in some cases."[38] What then is the most straightforward meaning? In Sanskrit, *ayurveda* means "knowledge of life and longevity."[39] This form of medicine connects our bodies with the whole of the cosmos. We are not separate from nature, but a part of it, even a microcosm of it.

Coward also writes about *ayurveda*,

> To study the health of the Hindu bather who goes to the river at daybreak, one must include the mantras chanted, the purifying experience of the body in water, the vegetarian *sattvic* quality of the food eaten, and so on—a gestalt of human-within nature/culture/religion analysis.

This is a wholistic view of health. And many Hindus throughout the world, and including in the United States, practice *ayurveda* with modern western medicine. Two specialists in *ayurveda*, D.P. Agrawal and Lalit Tiwati have commented,

> Today, Ayurveda is increasingly popular because it speaks of those elementary concepts of (1) contact with nature, (2) holism, and (3) we are what we eat . . . . The ultimate goal of Ayurveda is to help the individual discover a personal knowledge of living.[40]

Naturally, these themes not only find resonance with current wholistic approaches to medicine and health. It also does not entirely fit within the confines of western medicine.

Ethics, global climate change

As Menon emphasizes in the summary of Hinduism and science and highlights a key ethical term: "*Ahimsa* is non-injury and non-violent disagreement. The ideology behind *ahimsa* is 'to agree to disagree' and 'respect for differences.'" She continues with the wider meanings of term that relate more directly to science, *ahimsa* "can be interpreted in different ways, as 'respect for differences,' 'coexistence,' 'peaceful resolution of conflicts,' 'multi-dimensional perspectives,' 'learning from each others' experiences,' 'humility,' or 'ecological harmony of all life forms.'"[41]

Obviously, harming other animals for the sake of scientific research is problematic. Pollution of the environment is another by science and technology is another. As Coward writes,

> Hindu texts speak of a close relationship between dharma (right-eousness, duty, justice) and the ravaging of the earth. When dharma declines, humans take it out on nature. Modern science and technology, introduced into India during the British colonization and fostered by Jawaharlal Nehru's plans to industrialize India (undertaken after Indian attained independence in 1947), have led to serious pollution of the rivers, land, and air. This has been made worse by the country's population explosion and the desire of India's well-off classes (estimated at 200 to 250 million people) to consume conspicuously. This overpopulation and overconsumption has led to serious environmental degradation and an ecological crisis.[42]

The key for modern India, as also for the United States, is how to create sustainable science and technology and to resist climate change and broader environmental degradation. And the Hindu texts, like the Bhagavad Gita, can be seen as calls to action.

> Hindu gurus have begun to cite previously obscure texts such as "one tree is equal to ten sons." When political officials visit the temple they are given a tree to plant as a symbol that all trees are worthy of respect as part of God's body.[43]

Seeing the world as God's body, or put another way, that the divine is imminent in creation—or even that nature is divine—is powerful. In my teaching and lecturing, I have often expressed my conviction that the west has much to learn from religious traditions that emphasize the divine in nature. And yet, there is inevitably more nuance. I recall one of my best students at Chico State responding to a lecture I gave at Chico State's annual sustainability conference on this.[44] She pointed me to the book by Professor of Religious Studies at Indiana University. David Haberman, *River of Love in an Age of Pollution: The Yamuna River of Northern India.*[45] Haberman talked with those who held the river as sacred goddess and mother. I will paraphrase what I learned: They described three different views of the destruction: (1) since the river is a goddess, it is impossible to pollute her; (2) the river is polluted and that harms people, but the goddess is not affected; (3) our mother is sick, and it is imperative to care for her.

It appears that a sense of the divine in nature can lead to multiple viewpoints, not all of them promoting sustainability. Seek simplicity and distrust it, right? Still, as whole, Hinduism upholds a strong environmental ethic based on its key ethic of *ahimsa* and sacred texts.

Final thoughts

Subbarayappa offers this summary, tying together Hinduism, science, and the formation of the modern state of India: "Scientific attitudes and secularism—with equal respect for all religions—are among the guiding principles of the *Constitution of the Republic of India* (adopted soon after Independence) in recognition of the complementarity of science and religion for meaningful life."[46] Certainly, this is an important and defensible position. It is similarly echoed by physicist George Sudarshan, "In the Hindu tradition . . . the spiritual quest is in fact not distinct from the scientific, aesthetic or, for that matter, any academic pursuit."[47]

Hinduism has much to offer in its engagement with science. At the same time, for those who seek a non-western approach in approaching science, Hinduism is often overshadowed by Buddhism. Nevertheless, Hinduism influences how we understand science at least indirectly, channeled through cultural locations—like university research and the high-tech fields—where American Hindus predominate. Indeed, we can see connections both old and new between Hinduism and science that would seem to extend into the future as well.

Suggestions for further reading

I can recommend some excellent resources on Hinduism and science. To start with technology, I enjoyed the variety of approaches in the collected essays edited by Xenia Zeiler, *Digital Hinduism* (New York: Routledge Press, 2019). For a broader view of Hinduism and science, the collection edited by Makarand Paranjape is really useful, *Science, Spirituality and the Modernization of India* (New Delhi: Anthem, 2009). In addition, here I'd like to suggest some clear and succinct summaries: Howard Coward, "Hinduism, Contemporary Issues in Science and Religion," in *Encyclopedia of Science and Religion*, ed. J. Wentzel Vrede van Huyssteen (New York: Macmillan, 2003); Sangeetha Menon, "Hinduism and Science," in *The Oxford Handbook of Religion and Science*, eds. Philip Clayton and Zachary Simpson (Oxford: Oxford University Press, 2006); and B. V. Subbarayappa, "Indic Religions," in *Science and Religion around the World*, eds. John Hedley Brooke and Ronald L. Numbers (Oxford: Oxford University Press, 2011). That should get you started.

Notes

1 Dipanakar Gupta, "Why Hinduism Is Science Proof," 8 November 2010, *Times of India*, https://timesofindia.indiatimes.com/edit-page/why-hinduism-is-science-proof/articleshow/6884126.cms, accessed 16 June 2022.
2 Elaine Howard Ecklund, David R. Johnson, Brandon Vaidyanathan, Kirstin R.W. Matthews, Steven W. Lewis, Robert A. Thomson, Jr., Di Di, *Secularity and Science: What Scientists Around the World Really Think About Religion* (Oxford: Oxford University Press, 2019), 1.
3 Pew Trust, "On the Intersection of Science and Religion," 9 February 2021, www.pewtrusts.org/en/trend/archive/winter-2021/on-the-intersection-of-science-and-religion, accessed 16 June 2022.
4 B. V. Subbarayappa, "Indic Religions," in *Science and Religion around the World*, eds. John Hedley Brooke and Ronald L. Numbers (Oxford: Oxford University Press, 2011), 195.
5 PRRI, "The 2020 Census of American Religion," 8 July 2021, www.prri.org/research/2020-census-of-american-religion, accessed 21 May 2022.
6 "Hindus in American Textbooks," https://rpl.hds.harvard.edu/religion-context/case-studies/minority-america/hindus-american-textbooks; cf. www.immigration-research.org/indian-immigrants-in-the-united-states, both accessed 16 June 2022.
7 Pew Research Center, "Indians in the U.S. Fact Sheet," 29 April 2021, www.pewresearch.org/social-trends/fact-sheet/asian-americans-indians-in-the-u-s, accessed 16 June 2022.
8 "Indian Immigrants in the United States," 16 October 2020, www.migrationpolicy.org/article/indian-immigrants-united-states-2019#Age_education_employment, accessed 16 June 2022.
9 Christopher Southgate et al., *God, Humanity and the Cosmos*, 2nd ed. (Edinburgh: T&T Clark, 2005), 246; citing R. Guénon, *Man and His Becoming According to the Vedanta* (New York: Noonday Press, 1958), 25.
10 Philip Clayton, *Religion and Science: The Basics*, 2nd ed. (New York: Routledge Press, 2019), 48.
11 "Interview: Victoria Price," 3 May 2021, https://phdstudentstofollow.wordpress.com/2021/05/03/interview-victoria-price, accessed 9 July 2022.
12 Thoreau, *Walden*, www.literaturepage.com/read/walden-223.html, accessed 16 June 2022.
13 P. C. Ray, in John Hedley Brooke and Ronald L. Numbers, eds., *Science and Religion around the World* (Oxford: Oxford University Press, 2011), 203.
14 Subbarayappa, 197.
15 Makarand Paranjape, "Science, Spirituality and Modernity in India," in *Science, Spirituality and the Modernization of India*, ed. Makarand Paranjape (New Delhi: Anthem, 2008), 3.
16 Ibid., 13.
17 Klostermaier, "Hinduis, History of Science and Religion," in *Encyclopedia of Science and Religion*, ed. J. Wentzel Vrede van Huyssteen (New York: Macmillan, 2003), 405.
18 C. Mackenzie Brown, "Hindu Responses to Darwinism: Assimilation and Rejection in a Colonial and Post-Colonial Context," *Science and Education* 19 (2010): 705–38.
19 Pew, "On the Intersection of Science and Religion," 9 February 2021, www.pewtrusts.org/en/trend/archive/winter-2021/on-the-intersection-of-science-and-religion, accessed 16 June 2022.

20 Quoted in Brown, "Hindu Responses to Darwinism."

21 See the book of the same name edited by Xenia Zeiler, *Digital Hinduism* (New York: Routledge Press, 2020).

22 "Religion Among Scientists in International Context" **or** RASIC, https://rplp.rice.edu/research-studies/religion-among-scientists-international-context, accessed 16 June 2022.

23 Antoinette Elizabeth DeNapoli, "'Dharm Is Technology': The Theologizing of Technology in the Experimental Hinduism of Renouncers in Contemporary North India," *International Journal of Dharma Studies* 5 (2017): 18, https://internationaljournaldharmastudies.springeropen.com/track/pdf/10.1186/s40613-017-0053-0.pdf, accessed 16 June 2022.

24 Hanna Mannila and Xenia Zeiler, "Mediatized Gurus: Hindu Religious and Artistic Authority and Digital Culture," in *Digital Hinduism*, ed. Xenia Zeiler (New York: Routledge, 2020), 145–59.

25 Ibid., 159.

26 Huston Smith, *The World's Religions* (New York: Harper SanFrancisco, 1991), 68.

27 *Oxford Handbook*, 14, citing Sagan, *Cosmos* (New York: Random House, 1980), 32.

28 Tomoko Yoshida and Stephen P. Weldon, "Asian Traditions," in *Science and Religion: A Historical Introduction*, 2nd ed., ed. Gary B. Ferngren (Baltimore, MD: Johns Hopkins University Press, 2022), 317–8.

29 Subbarayappa, "Indic Religions," 195.

30 Harold Coward, "Hinduism, Contemporary Issues in Science and Religion," in *Encyclopedia of Science and Religion*, ed. J. Wentzel Vrede van Huyssteen (New York: Macmillan, 2003), 401–2.

31 Menon, "Indic Religions," in *Science and Religion around the World*, eds. John Hedley Brooke and Ronald L. Numbers (Oxford: Oxford University Press, 2011), 14.

32 Coward, "Hinduism," 402.

33 Menon, 14.

34 Daniel Gold, "Organized Hinduisms," in *Fundamentalisms Observed*, eds. Martin E. Marty and R. Scott Appleby (Chicago, IL: University of Chicago Press, 1991), 542–3; quoted in van Woorst, 26.

35 Menon, 13.

36 Clayton, 50.

37 Menon, 50.

38 Paranjape, "Science, Spirituality and Modernity in India," 5.

39 Gregory P. Fields, *Religious Therapeutics: Body and Health in Yoga, Ayurveda, and Tantra* (Albany, NY: SUNY Press, 2001), 36.

40 "Ayurveda: the Traditional Indian Medicine System and Its Global Dissemination," https://indicmandala.com/ayurveda-the-traditional-indian-medicine, accessed 16 June 2022.

41 Menon, "Indic Religions," in *Science and Religion Around the World*, eds. John Hedley Brooke and Ronald L. Numbers (Oxford: Oxford University Press, 2011), 9.

42 Coward, 403.

43 Ibid.

44 For example, Cootsona, "Too Heavenly Minded to Be of Earthly Good? Religious Views on Sustainability," talk at Chico State "This Way to Sustainability" Conference, 27 March 2020.

45 David Haberman, *River of Love in an Age of Pollution: The Yamuna River of Northern India* (Berkeley, CA: University of California Press, 2006).
46 Subbarayappa, "Indic Religions," 206.
47 George Sudarshan, "One Quest, One Knowledge," in *Science and the Spiritual Quest*, eds. W. Mark Richardson, et al. (London: Routledge, 2002), 252; cited in Clayton, 52.

9 Conclusion

Reflections on method and more

Science and lived religion often meet head-on. I have seen such a meeting at the hospital from which I construct two imaginary, but true, examples. Let's picture two pious Christian families hearing two different results. First:

> We prayed that John would be healed—I mean, we got our whole church to circle the entire hospital in a prayer vigil. But the doctor just told us, "The medical tests don't look good. You might want to talk about funeral arrangements." Where is God—who tells me in the Bible, "Ask and you shall receive"? I'm not sure I can it believe anymore. I've stopped praying.

And so begins a process where the assurance of faith gives way to the clarity of medical science.

A second scenario:

> Last month, the doctors gave Rebecca just six months to live because the cancer had spread throughout her body. But our small group prayed with us for several days and nights. And today, we just heard that the scans are clear! It's obvious that God is working in ways that science can't understand. God is good!

If it needs to be said (and perhaps it does), I don't recount these scenarios to belittle religious piety, but only to indicate how active religious practice can interact with the realities of science. I've already mentioned that I'm fascinated by the way in which cultural forces we call "scientific" and others we name "religious" interact has a stunning variety. What does a pious Muslim in Dar Es Salaam think about scientific procedures for fertility? How does a citizen in Beijing bring Buddhist ideas to bear on the technology and particularly the surveillance of her country? Does an

DOI: 10.4324/9781003214236-9

Adventist in Paradise, California advocate for new policies in light of the science of climate change after the devastating Camp Fire of 2018 and the nearby Dixie Fire of 2021?

One key, related conviction is that I don't want to fly so high that I lose sight of lived religion. My friend and colleague Yunus Dogan Telliel was very clear on this. And it's a temptation for scholars, like me, who love the interplay of ideas. But what does science and religious life mean for most people? Often, they are simply not in play together. Instead, we simply succumb to technology. We live with the iPhone in hand directing our lives and our thought—by some accounts, about five hours a day.[1] We gaze at them, almost as sacred oracles, in order to discern our relationship with self and the world.

As I wrote this book—and as I've done research over the past decade or so before actually writing—I've pondered the particularly salient lessons along the way. And this brings me to a concession. Frankly, most people—except for the rare breed of specialists—like to talk about method and thus engage in *methodology*, which is something I'm about to do. But I think is more interesting to consider one's method *after* rather than *before* reading the main chapters in the book. And so, my approach in this book has been to work at lived religious realities, and thus to include ethics, and not focus solely on systematic knowledge claims.

(By the way, I'd also like to introduce you to a new scholar, but in fact, there is no additional scholar for this chapter—I'm going to blame this conclusion all on me.)

Still on a crash course

Since this book focuses on the relationship of science with various religions in the United States and how they relate to science and religion frames the chapters, I'd like to return to what I wrote earlier on the study of religion. This has its own fascinating history and development.

The great commentator on religion and architect of the twentieth-century study of religion, the Harvard philosopher William James wrote,

> Were one asked to characterize the life of religion in the broadest and most general terms possible, one might say that it consists of the belief that there is an unseen order, and our supreme good lies in harmoniously adjusting ourselves thereto.[2]

His insights are so luminescent we still bask in their light.

And so, James's insights infer two questions that we have to answer (and I repeat): (1) Why is religion so widespread?[3] Augustine, in the fourth century CE, stated it succinctly as a prayer, "Lord, you created us for yourself, and our hearts are restless until they rest in you."[4] In a similar, often more secularized mode, the Cognitive Science of Religion agrees.[5] (2) On the other hand, why are religions so different? This in fact one common cavil against religious belief: "If religions point to the same Reality, why do they say such different and contradictory things?"

The 1893 World Parliament of Religions signaled that religious diversity well over a hundred years ago—which really in the United States, meant something beyond Protestant Christianity—was on our soil and is here to stay. The influx from Catholic countries and Chinese immigrants in the late nineteenth century, and Jewish immigrants later all brought religious pluralism. This increase in religious pluralism has only accelerated. And in the twenty-first century, the sheer numbers of religious people in the world lead to another reflection: If anything has come clear, it's the dizzying diversity of this conversation, particularly at the level at which most religious believers live.

Here then is a somewhat more leisurely tour of how these questions have been answered so that you know how I approach it. I've noted three phases in how post-Enlightenment scholars have approached religion. Yale professor of religion George Lindbeck[6] set out the conversation in a fresh way that has been too little appreciated by religious studies scholars.

First of all, the doctrinal or "propositional" approach tells us how well religious teachings refer objectively to reality, either here on the earth or in another realm or dimension like "heaven." Second, there is the experiential-expressive approach. It builds on eighteenth-century theologian-philosopher Friedrich Schleiermacher's well-known "feeling of absolute dependence,"[7] which connects with Huston Smith's *The World's Religions*, first published in 1958.[8] It clearly answers the question of why religion is widespread. Still, Lindbeck's criticism is incisive, "The datum that all religions recommend something which can be called 'love' toward that which is taken to be most important ('God') is a banality as uninteresting as the fact that all languages are (or were) spoken."[9] I'm not sure if everyone is as irritated as I am when someone tells me "we're essentially saying the same thing," when it's patently not true, and that person is effectively asserting their righteous opinion. It's passive–aggressive dominance.

With that in mind, Lindbeck's third alternative, the "cultural–linguistic" approach fascinates me—though I'm quick to add I don't buy it wholesale: "religions are seen as comprehensive interpretive schemes, usually embodied in myths or narratives and heavily ritualized, which structure human experience and understanding of self and world."[10] This view reverses how we normally think of inner life and its outer expression. Lindbeck asserts that we start by practicing our religion in community, which forms our experience: "a religious experience and its expression are secondary and tertiary in a linguistic-cultural model."[11] He adds that this means religions aren't saying the same things or that they produce the same effects: "different religions seem in many cases to produce fundamentally divergent depth experiences of what it is to be human."[12]

In understanding another's religion, we must respect differences and not amalgamate them. As Lindbeck writes with succinctness, "Adherents of different religions do not diversely thematize the same experience; rather they have different experiences."[13] Interreligious work is fundamentally translation, and as a student of comparative literature—and thus at least a handful of languages—translation is never precise. Or to quote what I heard in almost every comparative lit class, *traduttore, traditore*, or "The translator is a betrayer."

When Stephen Prothero picked up this approach with his book appropriately title, *God is Not One* (written over 50 years after Smith's first appearance), he is reflecting on what we now understand about pluralism. With racial diversity, we know this: "Don't call yourself 'colorblind' because that obscures the history of racism." Similarly, we need to be hold a similar concern in the study of religion because, as Prothero emphasizes, religions seek to answer particular questions. And those questions—and thus the answers—markedly differ. "The world's religious rivals do converge when it comes to ethics, but they diverge sharply when it comes to doctrine, ritual, mythology, experience, and law."[14] To assert that they all ultimately are one is "dangerous, disrespectful, and untrue."[15]

Need I add that this approach does imply asserting one religion's superiority over another? It does imply, though, that religions cannot be entirely compared with each other. To use the technical term, they are "incommensurable" languages.

> In short, the cultural-linguistic approach is open to the possibility that different religions and/or philosophies may have incommensurable notions of truth, of experience, and of categorical adequacy, and therefore also for what it would mean for something to be most important (i.e., "God").[16]

They are words in German, like *Gemuetlichkeit* or *Weltanschauung* that simply don't have the same meaning when translated into English, even if we use definitions like "a state or feeling of happiness, warmth, community, and good cheer" or "worldview."

I've already mentioned that, in this third phase of the study of religion, Prothero's contribution (and those like him) is significant. Nevertheless, I am not a disciple, and my own view veers toward a synthesizing of the strengths—and rejection of the weaknesses—of all three views. We need to address ways that religions assert truth. For example, I've never been able to figure out how both resurrection and reincarnation can coexist. Similarly, it's hard to deny that the majority of humanity has religious yearnings.[17] (But of course, what do we do with the over 1 billion atheists and agnostics in the world?)

In this book, I'm walking down a modified third roadway, and I hope these comments clarify why I've chosen that path.

Returning to the central topic

At the beginning of this book, I offered working definitions for science, religion, and technology. They worked well enough and were sufficiently simple. Now it's time to make things more complicated via history. (I am rephrasing here what I wrote in a much longer book, which unveils the history of science and religion in our country, *Negotiating Science and Religion in America.*[18])

Even in the title of this book, I'm writing as if I wrote as if *religion* and *science* represent two things or even two sets of things. The problem here is that neither *science* nor *religion* enjoys a particularly stable definition. In his book introducing readers to the study of the two and how they relate, Thomas Dixon has commented rather provocatively and with insight: "There has certainly not been a single and unchanging relationship between two entities called 'science' and 'religion.'"[19] To my mind, that makes this book more necessary, and the conversation about science and religion interesting.

Beginning with *science*, it did not exist as a discrete field for most of American history (and of course for centuries before that). Scholars (and others) used the Latin word for knowledge, *scientia*, for a variety of disciplines. Science today was called *natural philosophy* two hundred years ago. And the shift had collateral results. Johns Hopkins professor Lawrence Principe offered this succinct analysis:

> Natural philosophy is closely related to what we familiarly call *science* today, but is broader in scope and intent. The natural philosopher of the Middle Ages or the Scientific Revolution studied the natural world—as modern scientists do—but did so within a wider vision that included theology and metaphysics. The three components of God, man, and nature were never insulated from one another.[20]

I'm not sure most commentators understand how significant this is and how it happened.

In 1833, the Cambridge University historian and philosopher William Whewell coined the term *scientist* as replacement for terms like *cultivators of science*. Science with a capital S became reified in English. French and other languages refer to "the sciences" (or *les sciences*) or the "science of x," such as physics, biology, and—among some (like the Scottish theologian who was quite literate scientifically, Thomas Torrance)—even the "science of theology." In his *Studies in the History and Methods of Sciences*, A.D. Ritchie offers that "there is no Science in the singular, for there are only sciences."[21] And, "There is no one scientific method that is universally applicable."[22]

This signals the failure of the Logical Positivists in the 1920s to support their model of *verification*, as well as Karl Popper's later revision, yet also failure, to promote *falsification*. Either of these would have supported a hegemony of science, but they did not succeed, and what we learned in fourth grade as the "scientific method" ultimately fails to provide any real aid in grasping what scientists actually do. By the middle of the twentieth-century Thomas Kuhn's "paradigm shifts"[23] and Paul Feyerabend's *Against Method* (a book title that aptly describes its ethos and tone),[24] further solidify pluralism in the philosophies of science, which mirrors Prothero's approach to religion.

I could say more, but I hope I've given enough detail to undergird why I believe there is complexity to the word *science*. The science that we generally talk about is modern science, the science developed in sixteenth- and seventeenth-century Europe after Copernicus and Galileo. That's not always the way that different religions look at what we might think of as a connection with the natural world and another desire to understand that natural world. For example, Gregory Cajete says that, for Indigenous religions, especially Native American religions, there's a Native science that differs from modern science. It is not completely inconsistent with it, but different.

Historian of science and religion Peter Harrison has argued persuasively that some definitions that we take for granted have only existed in the past three hundred years or so. Harrison prefers to talk about the "territories" of religion and science, not their definitions.[25] Partly, this is a rejection that religion and science are "things," with *essences*, and thus that they can be reified. In philosophy, this is question of *essentialism*. Samford University Professor of Science and Religion Josh Reeves has raised the question of whether there are enduring essences in religion and science, or put another way, whether these two are *natural kinds*, that is, one that exists in nature and not simply in the socially constructed world of human beings. "To say that a kind is *natural* is to say that it corresponds to a grouping that reflects the structure of the natural world rather than the interests and actions of human beings."[26] Religion and science seem to lack essences and therefore are not natural kinds.

If religion is a "thing," then all who participate in this "thing," *ipso facto* agree. Indeed, it's not that simple. Religion, like truth, resists simplicity.[27] As I've said, my hope is to live by a kind of Academic Hippocratic Oath: *Do no harm*, to which I've added, *and seek to give enough vocabulary for others to enter this conversation with competency*. As Harrison noted, religion is that general topic that seems to have emerged as its own discrete word different from "piety" sometime in the 1800s. Religion in the singular developed from many voices, especially the twentieth-century religious studies giant Mircea Eliade (who effectively created the field of comparative religion as an academic discipline). It affirms that we are all religious. We all have a basic religious urge that's expressed in different perhaps traditions or religions. Many today adopt *spirituality* as an alternative and say, "I don't need to fall into the patterns, and the structures of and the institutions of a religion, I would rather look towards spirituality." I've decided instead to use the traditional term *religion*, and thus *religions*, to help define and, in some way, to give categories for various ways that people practice spirituality.

Perhaps, this is simply redundant, but with these nuances in mind, I still opted to move forward in the book with the following three definitions (which I have tested in teaching and writing over the past decades). I've cobbled these together from a variety of sources (e.g., Prothero, Smith). Still, the sources for my definition aren't responsible, but neither is it an entirely *de novo* creation from my brain. I repeat them here because they might sound a bit different after reading the preceding pages.

I defined *science* as "knowledge about or study of the natural world, framed in theories based on observation, which are tested through experimentation." Science studies nature. *Religion*, an even wilier term than science, doesn't just "study God," but can be defined as "the belief in God or in many gods or Ultimate Reality, as well as an organized system of beliefs, ceremonies, sacred stories, and ethical guidelines used to relate to God, a plurality of gods, or Ultimate Reality." Finally, I offered this definition *technology*, "the use of science in industry, engineering, etc. to invent useful things or to solve problems" and "a machine, piece of equipment, method, etc., that is created by the use of science."[28]

Reflections on related themes

A few related themes come to mind as I bring this book to a close.

First of all, and potentially violating my personal rule of not stating what is absolutely obvious, the sheer numbers involved in considering religious people in the world make it astoundingly complicated to summarize the conversation between science and religions. My introduction to religion students have heard me say, in a lecture on Islam, for example, "I'm offering general contours for the religion as a whole, but they shouldn't think that this applies to every single 1.8 billion Muslims."

Scholars have by now seen that I'm not seeking to break new ground in relating science and religions. In this brief treatment of various religions and science, I've not been able to represent the full range of the intricacies that scholars of religions present. Instead, I've tried to find the consensus views. Nonetheless, what is new is laying out all these religions in their interaction with science in an accessible way—in my research, I have not found any similar attempt. (This might have given me pause! Is it ultimately a fool's task?)

I might have been led to despair: *How can we say anything?* Our rocks of conviction and insight about science and religions may seem to be created from sand that slips through our grasp. I don't fall into despondency, and I hope you won't either. I believe we can say *something* about science and religions, but not *everything*. We can make definitive statements, but not they are always provisional and asymptotic. To return to the image employed by Lindbeck, religions are languages, and there is no universal language—no Esperanto—that perfectly translates all others.

All this adds up to something that makes my initial task complicated but worth the effort: I wanted to give you, as readers, some basic literacy in science and religions. But once you learn the basics of tennis, you soon realize that not everything is "turn (your body), step (into the stroke in the direction of the ball) and hit." That worked for the beginning, but as you got into competitive matches, it no longer is enough. It's now obvious that there is no easy way to relate any religious tradition seamlessly to science. Though many in the United States have heard that Christianity is anti-science and that Buddhism is maximally compatible with science, those slogans wear thin after reasonably minimal use.

My final take

After studying and working in the area of science and religion for a few decades, my own vision is largely for collaboration and/or integration between the two. It makes the most sense to me. Practically, it means we can have a more unified discourse about important values. Wouldn't we be better off as a country and a culture if these two titanic forces could get along? For me integration is also deeply human—each of us is after all one person, and whatever aspect of our lives is drawn to science or religion, they need to be integrated.

There are also significant challenges to seeking collaboration that emerge from the diversity of the religious perspectives and striking and sometimes challenging discoveries of science, but there is also the problem of apathy. One saying I found during a related internet search has this—beneath a picture of a beautiful beach at sunset reads the caption "Science vs. Religion." And further below this appears: "You can argue all you want about photons and miracles. I'll be out here, with a cold beer and a BBQ grill . . . Not really waiting for an answer." Many people indeed don't care. And they continue with their lives.

At the same time, though I promote collaboration, I know that conflicts between science and religion do happen and do affect us as a country—when religious voices resist the scientific wisdom of vaccines during a pandemic, or when science and technology promise salvation. We also need a dose of independent coexistence when we realize that these really are different. I don't want a Buddhist priest or Protestant pastor in every scientific laboratory. Neither do we want scientists instructing Muslims how to pray on Friday at midday. And I can't be alone in this. Over the years, I've become increasingly aware of the *differences* between science and religion. A zooarchaeologist classifying animal bones is different from a religious scholar analyzing Sanskrit texts on the history of Mahayana Buddhism.

Out of a commitment to honesty, I've learned that there are some major differences. I've mentioned atheist scientists like Jerry Coyne and Richard Dawkins. They see a very deep divide between religion and science, and they assert that they rely on experimentation and rationality and that just doesn't seem to connect with many people who fit into a religious mindset. At the same time, many influential religious voices in our country are not particularly supportive of science. The leaders of the conservative Christian movement, like Jerry Falwell Junior or Franklin Graham, command the attention of multitudes while standing against much of modern science.

There is no easy record of science and religions that could categorize and summarize all people.

In the search for collaboration, it would be convenient to find a universal common thread of wisdom that all the greatest minds in science and religion seek. I would like to fully concur with the philosopher and scholar of mystical thinking Ken Wilbur, who commented when collecting the writings of founders of quantum mechanics, "they investigated the physical realm so intensely looking for answers, and when they didn't find these answers, they became metaphysical." Even more, he added, "These physicists became deep mystics not because of physics but because of the limitations of physics."[29]

I am drawn to what astrophysicist Marcelo Gleiser wrote (and I repeat),

> Scientists should engage with the mystery of existence, inspired by a deep sense of awe and filled with humility. If science is seen this way, many more will be ready to embrace it as one of the highest expressions of the human spirit.[30]

These comments from Gleiser do bring me to perhaps the best-known scientist of our time, Albert Einstein. (It's significant that to be "an Einstein" is synonymous with intellectual brilliance.) Einstein constantly sought to cultivate the "cosmic religious feeling" (a phrase he first coined in 1930 in an essay for the *New York Times*), "In my view, it is the most important function of art and science to awaken this feeling and keep alive in those who are receptive to it."[31] Einstein believed that religion and science, properly understood, found convergence in seeking the highest aims of humanity. And it is indeed hard to argue with a scientist of this prominence and intellectual acumen.

> The fairest thing we can experience is the mysterious. It is the fundamental emotion that stands at the cradle of true are and true science. He who knows it not and can no longer wonder, no longer feel amazement, is as good as dead, a snuffed-out candle.[32]

Now we're getting closer. This is beautiful, and I'd find some deep agreement with Einstein, who identified the searching expressed in these pages, which I'd phrase as questions that stand somewhere near the center of the human condition. Where is meaning? How do I fit with the world and particularly with my group? What gives me hope, power, love?

I am, however, simultaneously less than convinced by Einstein's philosophical and theological conclusions. He felt the need to move away from traditional religious structures, particularly a deity who would answer prayer, a personal God, One who would allow for free will. For my part, the best answers come from particular, and not a generalized, allegedly universal language. My hope is that this book provides richer, nuanced, specific set of vocabularies and grammars, even if those languages are not our own. If we learn some competency for how to think like a Buddhist when encountering cosmology, and how to speak Ohlone (metaphorically at least) when caring for the natural world, then we've arrived at something worthwhile.

In this, I've drawn from the insights of another scholar of religion, as well as colleague at Chico State, Kate McCarthy:

> Religious pluralism is a fact that will not go away. After many centuries of confident missionary proclamations of the coming triumph of one or another religious vision; and one century of liberal championing of a coming unity of world religions, it appears clear at the turn of this millennium that religious difference is a feature of our human situation with which we will be reckoning for a long time.[33]

And if it's true for religious pluralism, it is also so for the ongoing contributions of these religions with science and technology, which won't stop, but will continue to affect our lives. To gain some literacy on how to bring religions (in the plural) together with the panoply of scientific discoveries is no small task. And to contribute to the collaboration of science and religion is my hope.

If there are nuances and problems with this view, I also recognize there are some great scientists and religious leaders who find collaboration quite compelling. Here, I immediately think of Einstein, Pope Francis, the Dalai Lama, and Francis Collins, all of whom really did or do see something that unites the aspirations of science and of religion. For me, this is especially poignant and inspiring in Collins, who creates this collaboration out of the specific language he dreams and prays in, that of the Christian tradition. "I find that studying the natural world is an opportunity to observe the majesty, the elegance, the intricacy of God's creation."[34]

These great practitioners have sought connections between science and religion. They've sought to find similar values like beauty, meaning, and a desire to discover something beyond this natural world that brings hope and exalts our souls.

Maybe learning the languages of their discoveries helps us hear their voices more clearly. I think this is so if we don't entirely agree . . . and that it is a worthy endeavor indeed.

Suggestions for further reading

I've already mentioned this book, but it provides such a lively overview of science and religion, why not note it again? Steve Paulson, *Atoms and Eden: Conversations on Religion and Science* (Oxford: Oxford University Press, 2010). An absolute icon in the study of religion is William James, *The Varieties of Religious Experience: A Study in Human Nature*

(New York: Penguin, 1982). My approach to religion in this book has been informed—but not slavishly so—by George Lindbeck, *The Nature of Doctrine: Religion and Theology in a Postliberal Age* (Philadelphia, PA: Westminster Press, 1984) as well as Stephen Prothero's expertly written, *God Is Not One: The Eight Rival Religions That Run the World* (New York: HarperOne, 2010). For two specific instances of thought leaders who have delineated a deeply integrated collaboration between religion and science, I recommend Dalai Lama, *The Universe in a Single Atom: The Convergence of Science and Spirituality* (New York: Morgan Road Books, 2005) and Francis Collins, *The Language of God: A Scientist Presents Evidence for Belief* (New York: Free Press, 2007).

Notes

1 "People devote third of waking time to mobile apps," 12 January 2022, *BBC News*, www.bbc.com/news/technology-59952557, accessed 30 June 2022.
2 William James, *The Varieties of Religious Experience: A Study in Human Nature* (New York: Penguin, 1982).
3 Huston Smith, *The World's Religions* (New York: Harper SanFrancisco, 1991).
4 Augustine, *Confessions*, Book 1.
5 My chapter, "Science and the *Sensus Divinitatis*: The Promise and Problem of the Natural Knowledge of God," in *Connecting Faith and Science: Philosophical and Theological Inquiries*, Claremont Studies in Science and Religion (Claremont, CA: Claremont Press, 2017).
6 George Lindbeck, *The Nature of Doctrine: Religion and Theology in a Postliberal Age* (Philadelphia, PA: Westminster Press, 1984).
7 Friedrich Schleiermacher, *The Christian Faith*, H.R. MacKintosh and J.S. Stewart, eds. (Edinburgh: T&T Clark, 1989), passim.
8 Smith, *The World's Religions*.
9 Lindbeck, 42.
10 Ibid., 32.
11 Ibid., 39.
12 Ibid., 41.
13 Ibid., 40.
14 Prothero, *God Is Not One: The Eight Rival Religions That Run the World* (New York: HarperOne, 2010), 3.
15 Ibid., 3.
16 Lindbeck, 49.
17 See "Science and the *Sensus Divinitatis*."
18 Cootsona, *Negotiating Science and Religion in America: Past, Present, and Future* (New York: Routledge Press, 2020).
19 Dixon, *Science and Religion: A Very Short Introduction* (Oxford: Oxford University Press, 2008), 3.
20 Lawrence Principe, *The Scientific Revolution: A Very Short Introduction* (Oxford: Oxford University Press, 2011), 27.
21 Thomas Torrance, *Theological Science* (Oxford: Oxford University Press, 1969), 106.
22 Ibid., 107.

23 Thomas Kuhn, *The Structure of Scientific Revolution*, 4th ed. (Chicago, IL: University of Chicago Press, 2012 [1962]).

24 Paul Feyerabend, *Against Method*, 3rd ed. (London: Verso, 1993).

25 Peter Harrison, *The Territories of Science and Religion* (Chicago, IL: University of Chicago Press, 2015), ch. 1.

26 Cf. *Stanford Encyclopedia of Philosophy*, "Natural Kinds," 15 March 2007, https://plato.stanford.edu/entries/natural-kinds, https://plato.stanford.edu/entries/natural-kinds, accessed 31 July 2019; cf. Josh Reeves, *Against Methodology in Science and Religion: Recent Debates on Rationality and Theology*, Routledge Science and Religion Series (New York: Routledge, 2018), e.g., 122ff.

27 An adaptation of a phrase attributed to John Green, www.goodreads.com/quotes/335186-truth-resists-simplicity, accessed 16 June 2022.

28 "Technology," Merriam-Webster Dictionary, www.merriam-webster.com/dictionary/technology, accessed 16 June 2022.

29 Steve Paulson, *Atoms and Eden: Conversations on Religion and Science* (Oxford: Oxford University Press, 2010), 183.

30 Gleiser, "Science vs. God," https://bigthink.com/13-8/science-god-false-choice/?fbclid=IwAR0ZrgAq73_m_iMC-iMoLN4PdxjwcKq5cC68jCJzElK_P4EdEFDglTxwZjU, accessed 16 June 2022.

31 Cited by Jammer, *Einstein and Religion* (Princeton, NJ: Princeton University Press, 1999), 79.

32 Einstein, *The World as I See It* (New Delhi: Prabhat Prakashan, 2021), ch. 1.

33 Cf. Kate McCarthy, "Reckoning with Religious Difference: Models of Interreligious Moral Dialogue," in *Explorations in Global Ethics: Comparative Religious Ethics and Interreligious Dialogue*, eds. Summer B. Twigg and Bruce Grelle (Boulder, CO: Westview Press, 1998), 98.

34 Quoted in David van Biema, "God vs. Science," *Time* 168 (13 November 2006): 50.

10 Glossary of terms

I don't intend this as an exhaustive guide. Still, here are a few terms from the book that might be unknown to many readers and therefore in search of a glossary.

Anatman or anatta: The Buddhist teaching that we have no enduring soul or self.

Anthropic Principle: *See Fine-tuning, cosmic.*

Astrotheology: A revision of theology in light of the possibility of extraterrestrial life.

Big Bang cosmology: An extrapolation of Albert Einstein's theory of general relativity, first presented in 1915, which pointed to an expanding universe implying an initial singularity where time began.

Dones: Those who once were involved with a religious institution, but are no longer.

Entanglement (quantum physics): "When two particles link together in a certain way no matter how far apart they are in space" (Space.com).[1]

Exoplanet: Planets outside our solar system.

Evolution: The change in the heritable characteristics of a species over successive generations.

Faith: A virtue emphasized by the monotheism, especially Christianity, which essentially means reliance, fidelity, or trust (exemplified in the key New Testament Greek word *pistis*).

Fine-tuning, cosmic (also Anthropic Principle): Building on discrete, precisely calibrated parameters that produced the universe and allow for the emergence of conscious, moral creatures, it states that

DOI: 10.4324/9781003214236-10

the universe is fitted from its inception for the emergence of life in general and intelligent, moral life in particular (though not necessarily earthly carbon-based life or *Homo sapiens* even though "anthropic" comes from the Greek word for human being, *anthropos*).

Hadith: Muslim sacred texts, which present records of Muhammad's sayings and acts.

Hominid: The group consisting of all modern and extinct great apes, such as modern humans, chimpanzees, gorillas and orangutans, and their ancestors.

Hominin: The group consisting of modern humans, extinct human species, and all our immediate ancestors, including members of *Homo*, *Australopithecus*, *Paranthropus*, and *Ardipithecus*.

Kalam: Generally associated with Islam, a cosmological argument that the existence of a creation requires a Creator.

Methodological naturalism: The method by which modern science does its work—studying the natural causes and effects, as well as their laws.

Myth: In the sense that religious scholars employ it are meaningful stories, not fiction, or even lies, as the word is popularly used.

Nones: Those who respond with "none" when asked, "what is your religious affiliation?"

Nonlocality (quantum physics): "Where there is no such thing as place or distance."[2]

Occasionalism: A term generally associated with Islam, "events are the result of entities whose cause is God alone. . . . A human agent is properly said to be able to act only at the moment he or she actually performs the action; only at this instant [or occasion] does God create in the person the ability to perform it" (*The Oxford Dictionary of Islam*).[3]

Orthopraxis: A term often associated with Judaism, but not used exclusively there, it means right action.

Orthodoxy: Right belief, emphasized by Christianity with its Creeds.

Pantheism: The belief that God is everywhere throughout the universe and thus all is divine; related to monism (all is one).

Quran (also sometimes, Koran): A record of Muhammad's revelations between 610 and 632CE, which Muslims believe to be the very speech of God, spoken in Arabic.

Religion: Belief in God or in many gods or Ultimate Reality, as well as an organized system of beliefs, ceremonies, sacred stories, and ethical guidelines used to relate to God, a plurality of gods, or Ultimate Reality.

Science: Knowledge about or study of the natural world, framed in theories based on observation, which are tested through experimentation.

Scientific *tafsir*: The assertion that verses in the Quran contain facts and theories later discovered by modern science.

***Shoah*:** Hebrew for "catastrophe," another term for the Holocaust, the killing of 6 million European Jews by the Nazis.

Speciesism: The belief that human beings are unique and thus above all other animals.

Spiritual but Not Religious (SBNR): The growing demographic in the United States that do not affiliate with a religion but affirm a deep spiritual connection with the world around them and seek transcendence beyond the material world.

Technology: The use of science in industry, engineering, etc. to invent useful things or to solve problems and a machine, piece of equipment, method, etc., that is created by the use of science.

Talmud: Sacred Jewish writings, a record of the rabbinical oral tradition from several centuries that surround these writings in two collections, the Palestinian Talmud and the Babylonian from about 425 and 500 CE, respectively.

Tanakh: Another name for the Hebrew Bible that stands for its three parts, *Torah* (law or instruction), *Nevi'im* (Prophets), and *Ketuvim* (Writings).

Tawhid: "The defining doctrine of Islam—the unity and uniqueness of God as creator and sustainer of the universe" (*The Oxford Dictionary of Islam*).[4]

***Tikkun olam*:** The Hebrew phrase, which means "the healing of the world" and which guides Jewish ethics.

Transhumanism: A movement that promotes the ability of technology to help human beings transcend the limitations of biologically based life.

Notes

1 "Quantum entanglement: A simple explanation," www.space.com/31933-quantum-entanglement-action-at-a-distance.html, accessed 11 May 2022.

2 George Musser, "How Einstein Revealed the Universe's Strange "Nonlocality," 1 November 2015, *Scientific American*, www.scientificamerican.com/article/how-einstein-revealed-the-universe-s-strange-nonlocality, accessed 10 May 2022.

3 John L. Esposito, ed. *Oxford Dictionary of Islam* (Oxford: Oxford University Press, 2003), 239.

4 *The Oxford Dictionary of Islam*, 317.

Index

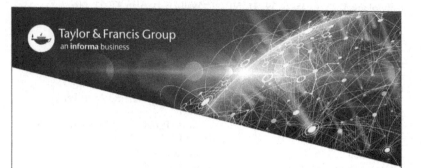